Investing Online
FOR
DUMMIES®
QUICK REFERENCE

by Thomas S. Gray

Wiley Publishing, Inc.

Investing Online For Dummies® Quick Reference

Published by
Wiley Publishing, Inc.
111 River Street
Hoboken, NJ 07030
www.wiley.com

Copyright © 1999 Wiley Publishing, Inc., Indianapolis, Indiana

Published simultaneously in Canada

For general information on our other products and services or to obtain technical support, please contact our Customer Care Department within the U.S. at 800-762-2974, outside the U.S. at 317-572-3993, or fax 317-572-4002.

Wiley also publishes its books in a variety of electronic formats. Some content that appears in print may not be available in electronic books.

Library of Congress Cataloging-in-Publication Data:
Library of Congress Control Number: 00-101529
ISBN: 0-7645-0716-8

10 9 8 7 6 5 4

About the Author

Thomas S. Gray is a journalist and author who has written on business, technology, and other fields for a number of publications, including the Los Angeles Times and TechWeek magazine. Born in Southern California, he was educated at Stanford University and UCLA, headed the editorial pages at the Daily News in Los Angeles, and later was senior editor at Investor's Business Daily. He is the author, with Claire Mencke, of IDG Books' *Teach Yourself Investing Online.* He lives in Oak Park, California with his wife, Barbara Bronson Gray, and their two children.

Dedication

To Barbara

Author's Acknowledgments

Online investing, like everything else on the Internet, is a subject that never stands still. Each day seems to bring a new look to one investor-oriented Web site and new tools to another. Keeping up with all this change and producing a timely guide is a challenge that requires a strong team of editors at the writer's side. I would like to thank all those at IDG Books who helped bring this book to fruition, especially Acquisitions Editor Laura Moss, who spearheaded this project and introduced me to it, and Darren Meiss, who steered the book through the writing and editing process. I'm also grateful to Development Editor Brian Kramer and Copy Editor Suzanne Thomas for their help in bringing this text to its final, polished form.

Finally — and certainly not as an afterthought — I owe a debt of gratitude to my wife, Barbara, and my children, Jonathan and Katie, for seeing me through this task with support, encouragement, and tolerance for long working hours and short weekends.

Publisher's Acknowledgments

We're proud of this book; please send us your comments through our Online Registration Form located at www.dummies.com/register

Some of the people who helped bring this book to market include the following:

Acquisitions, Editorial, and Media Development

Project Editor: Darren Meiss

Development Editor: Brian Kramer

Acquisitions Editor: Laura Moss

Copy Editor: Suzanne Thomas

Technical Editor: Gene Bednarek

Editorial Manager: Rev Mengle

Media Development Manager: Heather Heath Dismore

Editorial Assistant: Candace Nicholson

Production

Project Coordinator: Maridee Ennis

Layout and Graphics: Joe Bucki, Amy Adrian, Tracy K. Oliver, Jacque Schneider, Janet Seib, Brandon Yarwood,

Proofreaders: Laura Albert, York Production Services, Inc.

Indexer: York Production Services, Inc.

Special Help
Amanda M. Foxworth, Dwight Ramsey

General and Administrative

Wiley Technology Publishing Group: Richard Swadley, Vice President and Executive Group Publisher; Bob Ipsen, Vice President and Group Publisher; Joseph Wikert, Vice President and Publisher; Barry Pruett, Vice President and Publisher; Mary Bednarek, Editorial Director; Mary C. Corder, Editorial Director; Andy Cummings, Editorial Director

Wiley Manufacturing: Carol Tobin, Director of Manufacturing

Wiley Marketing: John Helmus, Assistant Vice President, Director of Marketing

Wiley Composition Services: Gerry Fahey, Vice President, Production Services; Debbie Stailey, Director of Composition Services

Contents at a Glance

Table of Contents

Investing Online

There's no place like a home page to see at a glance what the Internet can do for you as an investor. So, before rushing ahead to planning, quotes, research, trading, IPOs, and other parts of this book, take a few minutes to look at the Big Picture here, starting with some typical investor-oriented home pages.

In this part, you also find a description of toolbars and basic tasks in both Netscape Navigator (in version 4.72 of Communicator) and Microsoft Internet Explorer (version 5.0). The part ends by showing some of the cool — and useful — things an investor can do online, and where in this book you can find out more about them.

In this part . . .

- ✔ What You See
- ✔ Toolbar Table
- ✔ The Basics
- ✔ What You Can Do

What You See: An Investing Home Page

Here is the opening page of CNET Investor (www.cnetinvestor.com), one of many sites on the Web that package quotes, stock news, portfolio-tracking, and other investing tools. To find out more about the features highlighted here (and to see similar features at other online sites) check out the recommended part later in this book.

Market averages: see Part VI

Quotes and charts: see Part II

Company news: see Part III

Portfolio Tracking: see Part X

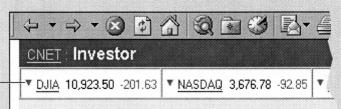

CNET · **Investor**

▼ DJIA 10,923.50 -201.63   ▼ NASDAQ 3,676.78 -92.85   ▼

Enter symbol: tstn   Fast Quote, News &

Tech News | Finance and Investing | **My Portfolio**

Sun's profit rises as sales jump 35

The company says third-quarter profit rose to $436 m share, as sales surged 35 percent to $4 billion.

Gateway's quarterly earnings rise 37 percent on sales from its services businesses.
Full story

inves

Market swings threaten start-ups

Companies are increasingly facing a tough audience of investors when raising capital.

CNET inv

Applied Ma trading with changing ha

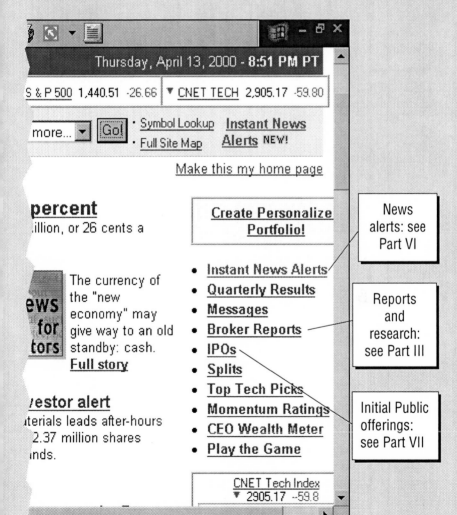

Thursday, April 13, 2000 - **8:51 PM PT**

S & P 500 1,440.51 -26.66 | ▼ CNET TECH 2,905.17 -59.80

more... ▼ Go! · Symbol Lookup **Instant News**
· Full Site Map **Alerts NEW!**

Make this my home page

percent
illion, or 26 cents a

Create Personalize Portfolio!

News alerts: see Part VI

The currency of the "new economy" may give way to an old standby: cash. **Full story**

- **Instant News Alerts**
- **Quarterly Results**
- **Messages**
- **Broker Reports**
- **IPOs**
- **Splits**
- **Top Tech Picks**
- **Momentum Ratings**
- **CEO Wealth Meter**
- **Play the Game**

Reports and research: see Part III

Initial Public offerings: see Part VII

estor alert
terials leads after-hours
2.37 million shares
nds.

CNET Tech Index
▼ 2905.17 --59.8

3

What You See: Two Popular Home Pages

The two sites shown on these two pages are among the most popular and full-featured sites.

The two sites are Yahoo! Finance (finance.yahoo.com), and American Online Personal Finance (for AOL subscribers, at the Personal Finance channel).

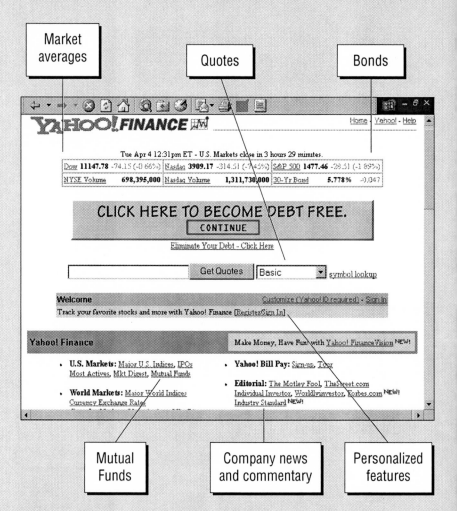

Market averages

Quotes

Bonds

Mutual Funds

Company news and commentary

Personalized features

Portfolio tracking

Quotes

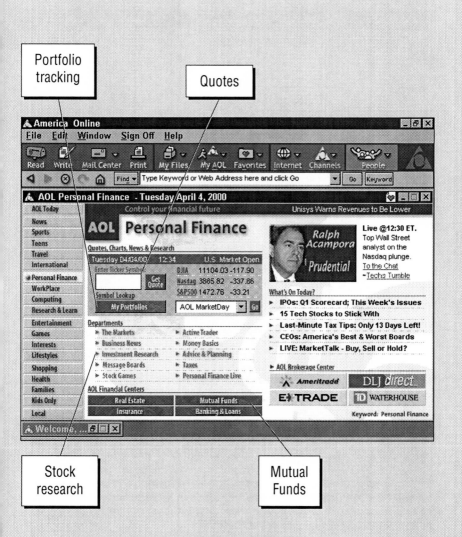

Stock research

Mutual Funds

Toolbar Table: Microsoft Internet Explorer

The following table shows key buttons on the Explorer and Address bars in Internet Explorer 5.0, with a description of the task they perform, keyboard shortcuts (if any), and references to other parts of The Big Picture where you can find out more about them.

Tool/Button	Name	What You Can Do	Shortcut	See
Back	Back	Return to the last page you viewed		
Forward	Forward	View the page you visited before you clicked the Back button		
Stop	Stop	Stop the download of a new Web page		
Refresh	Refresh	Get the latest version of the page you're viewing	Ctrl+R	
Home	Home	Return to your home page (the page that appears when you start the browser)		The Basics: Setting Up an Investor-Friendly Home Page
Search	Search	Open the search engine menu to look for a Web site	Ctrl+E	The Basics: Search Engines
Favorites	Favorites	Open a menu to bookmark the current site for future use and to recall sites saved earlier	Ctrl+I	The Basics: Bookmarking
History	History	Open a list of Web pages you have viewed recently	Ctrl+H	
Mail	Mail	Read and write e-mail		
Print	Print	Print the current Web page	Ctrl+P	

Toolbar Table: Netscape Navigator

The following table shows key buttons on the Navigation and Location toolbars in Netscape Navigator, with a description of the task they perform, keyboard shortcuts (if any), and references to other parts of The Big Picture where you can find out more about them.

Tool/ Button	Name	What You Can Do	Shortcut	See
Back	Back	Return to the last page you viewed		
Forward	Forward	View the page you visited before you clicked the Back button		
Reload	Reload	Get the latest version of the page you're viewing	Ctrl+R	
Home	Home	Return to your home page (the page that appears when you start your browser)	Ctrl+N	The Basics: Setting Up an Investor-Friendly Home Page
Search	Search	Use search engine(s) to find a Web page		The Basics: Search Engines
My Netscape	My Netscape	Go to the Netscape home page		
Print	Print	Print the current page	Ctrl+P	
Security	Security	Show security data on current page; change security settings		The Basics: Security Features
Stop	Stop	Stop the download of a new Web page		
Bookmarks	Bookmarks	Display or edit list of bookmarked Web pages	Ctrl+B	The Basics: Bookmarking

The Basics: Starting & Closing a Browser

To start a browser such as Microsoft Internet Explorer or Netscape Navigator, make your Internet connection first. If you use a modem and dial-up connection, the dialer program will include instructions for choosing and/or changing the default browser, which starts automatically when you log on to the Internet.

If you have a dial-up account with American Online, AOL's browser (a version of Internet Explorer) starts automatically. You can use it from any AOL screen by typing a Web address in the space just to the right of the Find button.

If you have an always-on Internet connection (through cable or DSL, for instance) start your browser by double-clicking its large icon on your desktop or its small icon in the taskbar.

Closing and switching browsers

Close a browser by clicking the Close box (X) at the top right-hand corner of the window. You can switch browsers by closing one and starting another using the desktop icon.

If you're logged on to AOL through a dial-up connection and want to use Netscape or the standard version of Internet Explorer, minimize (don't close) your AOL window by clicking the Minimize button. Then start your browser from a desktop icon.

The Basics: Typing Web Addresses

The most direct way to load a Web page is to type its address (URL, as it's technically known) in the toolbar just under the navigation buttons. In Navigator, this area is the Location Toolbar; if you don't see it, choose View⇨Show⇨ Location Toolbar. In Internet Explorer, type URLs into the Address Bar. If you don't see it, choose View⇨Toolbars⇨Address Bar.

Both browsers have similar steps for typing addresses:

1. Start by clicking the cursor in the Address Bar and pressing Delete to clear the address that's already there.

2. If you know the full URL, simply type it in and press Enter.

   If you know only part of the address (or are making an educated guess), type what you know, such as a company name, and press Enter.

   Both Navigator (shown later) and Internet Explorer are designed to search out the most likely sites to match your query.

See also "The Basics: Search Engines."

Typing addresses in AOL

From the AOL home page, you can type Web addresses in the field next to the Find button. Then click Go.

If the term you're using is an AOL keyword, you go to an AOL site. To search only the Web, click the Find button and choose Find It on the Web.

Recalling addresses

Navigator, Internet Explorer, and AOL browsers all store a limited number of previously-typed addresses in their Address or Location toolbar. Click the button to the right of the address line to pull down a list.

You see only Web addresses actually typed, not all of the sites you've visited (to see those, use the History button in the toolbar — **See also** the Toolbar Table sections earlier in this part). Note, too, that incorrect URLs also show up on this list if you've typed them and failed to find a site.

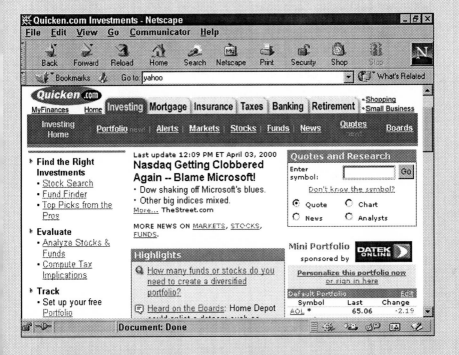

The Basics: Search Engines

Search engines, like automated librarians, take a word, phrase, or concept from you and comb the Internet to see what matches. You can choose (www.searchengineguide.com) listed 3,230 as of April 2000, with 380 in the Business category alone.

Because all of these hunters and gatherers are working the same territory, the World Wide Web, they end up duplicating one another quite a bit. So you don't have to use every one of them to cover the Web adequately. You should use at least a few of them regularly, however, because they don't all search in the same way or bring back the same results.

An effective way to search is to use multi-engine sites, such as Dogpile (www.dogpile.com) or MetaCrawler (www.metacrawler.com). These let you search simultaneously with a number of engines.

Searching with Navigator

The Search button in the Netscape Navigator toolbar calls up a directory of links to several popular search engines including Excite, GoTo.Com, HotBot, LookSmart, Lycos, and Netscape's own search program. You can search right away by doing the following:

1. Click the link for the search engine you want to use.

2. Type your search terms and press Enter.

You can check a box next to "Keep ... as My Search Engine" to make this engine the one always highlighted when you click the Search toolbar button. Other engines are listed as links below the main menu.

Searching with Internet Explorer

When you click the Search button in the Internet Explorer toolbar, a window opens to the left of your screen with a choice of search categories (Find a Web Page, Find a Business, and so forth). Then:

1. Use the radio buttons to pick a search category.

2. Type your query, as instructed on the screen, in the box just below the category list.

3. Click Search.

You can also use this window to customize your searches and choose which search engines Internet Explorer uses to find Web site matches from the Address bar. Click the Customize button to open a dialog box where you can make changes to the way Internet Explorer performs searches.

The Basics: Bookmarking

Bookmarks (called Favorites in Internet Explorer) are essential tools for keeping track of the many Web sites that you visit as an online investor. When you've called up a page you want to save for quick retrieval, follow these steps in Internet Explorer:

1. Click the Favorites toolbar button.

2. Click Add in the left-hand pane.

3. In the "Add Favorite" dialog box, click OK to add the page to the unsorted list. Or, if you want to add it to an existing folder, open the folder you want by clicking it.

4. Click OK.

In Navigator, add the Web page you're viewing to Navigator's bookmarks by clicking the Bookmarks button and choosing one of these options from the pull-down menu:

- ✔ Add Bookmark to save it in the unsorted list.
- ✔ File Bookmark to save it in an existing folder (a list of these will appear).

Favorites button

The Basics: Security Features

Online and off, you need to make sure your money and personal financial data are protected. On the Internet, sensitive information is sent in encrypted form to thwart eavesdropping. For any stock transactions, brokerage or bank account data, credit-card numbers, and similarly sensitive data, make sure you're sending it in 128-bit encryption, the highest level available.

Internet Explorer and Netscape Navigator both give you tools for checking the security at the Web page you're currently using:

- ✔ In Internet Explorer, a padlock icon (with the lock closed) appears in the status bar when you're on a secure page. Place your cursor on it to find out the encryption level.

- ✔ In both Internet Explorer and Navigator, the URL of a secure page will start with *https* rather than the usual "http." Check the address line for this.

In Netscape Navigator, the padlock logo on the Security toolbar button tells you whether the current page is encrypted. It's closed if the page is encrypted, open if it's not.

To get detailed information on your security level, click the Security button to see the window below. Check these items:

- ✔ **Encryption.** Navigator tells you if the current page is secure and explains what this security level means in practical terms (for example, whether other people could see it when you loaded it and whether you can check the identity of the Web site).

- ✔ **Certificate.** If the page is secure, you see a View Certificate button next to the Open Page Info button. Click View Certificate to see who holds the digital security certificate for the page you're viewing — it should match the name in the URL.

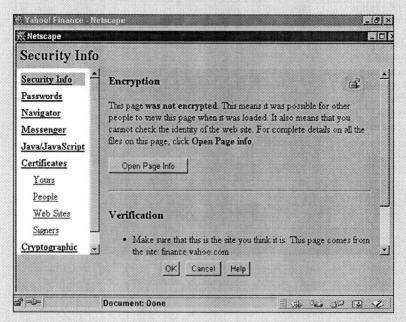

The Basics: Setting Up an Investor-Friendly Home Page

If you find yourself frequently returning to an investment-focused Web page to get quotes or check your portfolio, you may want to make that page the home page for your browser — the one that comes up first when the browser logs on to the Internet.

To specifying a home page in Netscape Navigator follow these easy steps:

1. Go to the Web page you want to use as the home page.
2. Choose Edit⇨Preferences.
3. Click Navigator in the left-hand pane.
4. Click the Home Page radio button.
5. Click Use Current Page.
6. Click OK to save your new settings.

To set the current page as a home page in Internet Explorer, choose Tools⇨ Internet Options. Then, click Use Current under Home Page and click OK.

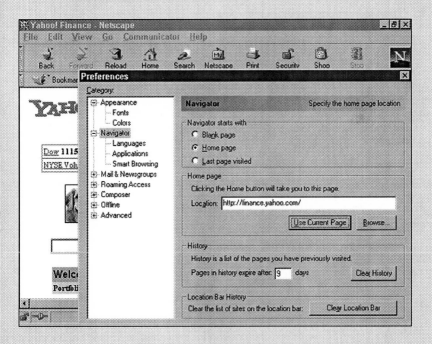

What You Can Do: Research a Stock

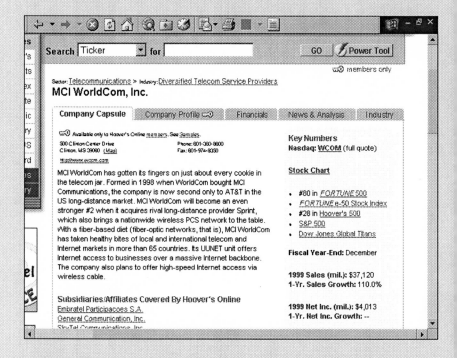

Search [Ticker ▼] for [　　　　　　　　　　] [GO] [⚡ Power Tool]

🔒⊙ members only

Sector: Telecommunications > Industry: Diversified Telecom Service Providers

MCI WorldCom, Inc.

| Company Capsule | Company Profile ⊙ | Financials | News & Analysis | Industry |

🔒⊙ Available only to Hoover's Online members. See Samples.

500 Clinton Center Drive
Clinton, MS 39060 (Map)
http://www.wcom.com

Phone: 601-360-8600
Fax: 601-974-8050

MCI WorldCom has gotten its fingers on just about every cookie in the telecom jar. Formed in 1998 when WorldCom bought MCI Communications, the company is now second only to AT&T in the US long-distance market. MCI WorldCom will become an even stronger #2 when it acquires rival long-distance provider Sprint, which also brings a nationwide wireless PCS network to the table. With a fiber-based diet (fiber-optic networks, that is), MCI WorldCom has taken healthy bites of local and international telecom and Internet markets in more than 65 countries. Its UUNET unit offers Internet access to businesses over a massive Internet backbone. The company also plans to offer high-speed Internet access via wireless cable.

Subsidiaries/Affiliates Covered By Hoover's Online
Embratel Participacoes S.A.
General Communication, Inc.
SkyTel Communications, Inc.

Key Numbers
Nasdaq: WCOM (full quote)

Stock Chart

- #80 in *FORTUNE* 500
- *FORTUNE* e-50 Stock Index
- #28 in Hoover's 500
- S&P 500
- Dow Jones Global Titans

Fiscal Year-End: December

1999 Sales (mil.): $37,120
1-Yr. Sales Growth: 110.0%

1999 Net Inc. (mil.): $4,013
1-Yr. Net Inc. Growth: --

Want to know more about that stock that caught your eye? Want to find some good stocks you may be missing? The Internet makes it easy to screen the universe of stocks for the ones that fit your strategy. And when it comes to researching companies, it can give you anything from a simple snapshot to a full-scale history and analysis of a publicly traded company.

The following is a quick guide to researching a stock:

Get started by:

✔ Screening for stocks that meet your criteria: **Part III**

✔ Calling up a company snapshot: **Part III**

✔ Calling up a quote and chart: **Part II**

Work on your project by:

- ✔ Comparing the company's financial performance with its own past and its industry peers: **Part III**

- ✔ Putting the company (and others) on a watch list: **Part X**

- ✔ Studying SEC filings: **Part III**

Add finishing touches by:

- ✔ Finding out what analysts are saying and company insiders are doing: **Part III**

- ✔ Reviewing your investment strategy to see if a particular stock still fits your strategy: **Part I**

- ✔ Setting up alerts to get the latest news on the stock: **Part VI**

What You Can Do: Buy and Sell Investments Online

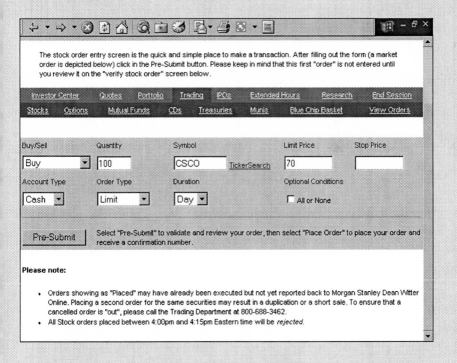

The stock order entry screen is the quick and simple place to make a transaction. After filling out the form (a market order is depicted below) click in the Pre-Submit button. Please keep in mind that this first "order" is not entered until you review it on the "verify stock order" screen below.

Investor Center	Quotes	Portfolio	Trading	IPOs	Extended Hours	Research	End Session
Stocks	Options	Mutual Funds	CDs	Treasuries	Munis	Blue Chip Basket	View Orders

Buy/Sell	Quantity	Symbol		Limit Price	Stop Price
Buy	100	CSCO	TickerSearch	70	

Account Type	Order Type	Duration	Optional Conditions
Cash	Limit	Day	☐ All or None

Pre-Submit — Select "Pre-Submit" to validate and review your order, then select "Place Order" to place your order and receive a confirmation number.

Please note:

- Orders showing as "Placed" may have already been executed but not yet reported back to Morgan Stanley Dean Witter Online. Placing a second order for the same securities may result in a duplication or a short sale. To ensure that a cancelled order is "out", please call the Trading Department at 800-688-3462.
- All Stock orders placed between 4:00pm and 4:15pm Eastern time will be *rejected*.

The Internet gives you the ability to place buy and sell orders in seconds on stocks, bonds, and mutual funds. It also helps you with the steps you must take first, such as planning your investment strategy and choosing a broker.

The following is a quick guide to buying and selling investments online, from start to finish.

Get started by:

- ✔ Creating an investment strategy to meet your needs: **Part I**
- ✔ Using online ratings and other resources to shop for a broker: **Part IV**
- ✔ Checking regulators to look for possible problems: **Part IV**

Work on your project by:

- ✔ Setting up a brokerage account online: **Part V**
- ✔ Researching mutual fund and bond sales online: **Part VIII**
- ✔ Finding companies that sell stock directly: **Part V**

Add finishing touches by:

- ✔ Looking for price and volume action that signals a time to buy or sell: **Part VI**
- ✔ Placing orders: **Part V**
- ✔ Confirming orders and keeping records: **Part V**

What You Can Do: Tracking a Portfolio

Online programs enable you to track your stocks and mutual funds with constantly updated prices and performance data. The following is a quick guide to using the Internet (along with desktop software) to track a portfolio:

Get started by:

- ✔ Customizing quotes to choose which data you'll track online: **Part II**
- ✔ Creating a new portfolio at an online financial site: **Part X**
- ✔ Adding securities that you already own to a new portfolio: **Part X**

Work on your project by:

> ✓ Recording new buys and sells: **Part X**
>
> ✓ Moving data between desktop software and online sites: **Part X**
>
> ✓ Setting up alerts to get news on securities you own: **Part VI**

Add finishing touches by:

> ✓ Using online tools to analyze your portfolio's performance and asset mix: **Part X**
>
> ✓ Reviewing your investment plan to see if your portfolio is on track: **Part I**
>
> ✓ Figuring your capital gains and taxes: **Part XI**

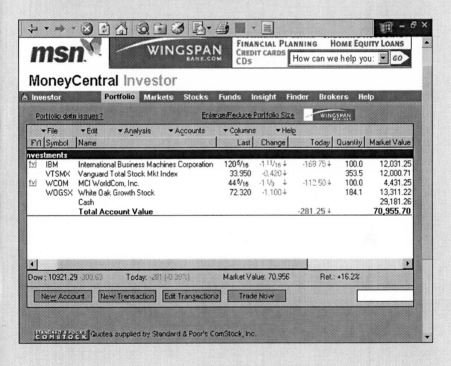

Part I

Creating Your Investment Plan

This part tells you how to determine your investment readiness and how to set financial goals by using online tools. It shows how Web sites can help you figure out what you need to save for retirement, college, and other life expenses. You also find sites that help you with *asset allocation* — finding the mix of stocks, bonds, and cash that is right for your needs and your risk tolerance.

In this part . . .

Allocating Assets

How much should you invest in stocks, bonds, or cash (such as savings accounts or money-market funds)? The answer to that question depends on a host of factors:

- ✔ How much money you have now

- ✔ How much money you'll need (near- and long-term)

- ✔ Your age

- ✔ Your comfort with risk

- ✔ Your expectations about the economy

No single formula fits everyone, but you can use interactive programs at several Web sites to get some idea of the asset mix that is right for you.

See also "The Big Picture" for more information on the basics of getting around on the Internet.

Asset allocation with SmartMoney

One of the easiest programs to use to figure out asset allocation is at the SmartMoney site (www.smartmoney.com/si/tools/oneasset). Go to the site and use the following steps.

1. In the section labeled Value of All Assets, Including Windfall, Invested In, fill in your current assets by category.

- *Cash* refers to money-market funds, savings accounts, and CDs.

- *Bonds* and *stocks* refer to mutual fund holdings as well as individual securities.

A pie chart showing your asset mix appears.

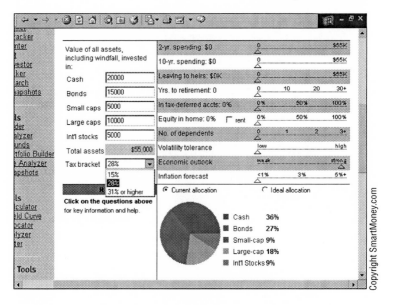

2. Enter your federal income tax bracket in the Tax Bracket field.

   If you're planning well into the future and you expect your income to go up or down significantly, try to estimate what your bracket will be in the coming years.

3. In the right-hand grid, adjust the pointers on each line (by clicking and dragging with the button on your mouse) to reflect your age, family obligations, and expected financial needs.

   For 2-yr. and 10-yr. spending, estimate how much of your assets (not current income) you'll need to spend over those periods of time.

   The line labeled Volatility Tolerance measures how you respond to sharp market downturns. Volatility tolerance is similar to risk tolerance, which you can measure at other Web sites. *See also* "Finding Your Investment Style" for more on risk tolerance.

   Money in tax-deferred accounts will be taxed as ordinary income when you finally use it.

4. Click the button labeled Ideal Allocation just above your allocation pie chart to see what the program recommends, based on your answers.

   A new pie chart appears, along with recommendations for changing your assets from the current mix.

5. Move any of the pointers to see how your recommended mix changes as your circumstances do.

The cash portion of the mix increases if you need more money in the two-year window. The small-cap category rises the further you are from retirement because more time allows for taking greater risk — like putting money into more volatile investments (such as small-cap stocks).

Asset allocation with ThirdAge

Go to the ThirdAge site (www.thirdage.com/features/money/allocator) for a quick look at suggested asset allocations based on your stage in life.

This site is especially good for middle-aged or retired investors.

1. On the Allocator page, choose one of four links after the question "At Which Stage of Life Are You?"

   A pie-chart with a suggested blend of stocks, bonds, and cash appears. An explanation of age-related factors that influence your portfolio appears over each chart. In general, the site recommends more cash and bond investment with age; although ThirdAge (and other advisors) recommends that you never totally get out of stocks.

2. Click the Conclusions link under any chart to go to more links, including an asset allocation forum where you can post questions and join in discussions (free registration required).

Asset allocation with Schwab's investor profile

The Charles Schwab Web (www.schwab.com) site has a wealth of investment planning tools that you can use even if you don't have a Schwab brokerage account.

1. At the Charles Schwab home page, click the Planning tab.

2. Click the Planning Tools link.

3. Go to Investor Profile.

4. At the Investor Profile questionnaire, use the pull-down menus to answer the questions about your investment needs, experience, and style.

   For the final question, choose a stock scenario (each has a different level of volatility and potential return) that suits your investment personality.

5. Click Send to get a recommended allocation based on your answers.

   You also get an assessment of your investment style, from conservative to aggressive.

Finding Your Investment Style

Determining your investment style or personality enables you to create a portfolio of stocks, bonds, funds, and/or cash. Determining how you cope with the risk of losing money, or your *risk tolerance,* can help you decide where you put your money and what returns you can expect.

Risk tolerance has two aspects:

✔ **Your wealth:** Your wealth is how much money you can really afford to put at risk and possibly lose.

✔ **Your frame of mind and your response to market volatility:** If your stocks suddenly dropped in value, would you panic, wait patiently, or go on a buying spree?

Various Web sites offer tools to help you figure out your investment style. *See also* "The Big Picture" for more information on the basics of getting around on the Internet.

Measuring risk tolerance at MSN

The risk tolerance quiz at MSN Investor (`www.moneycentral.investor.com/investor/home.asp`) covers the bases in helping you determine your investment style:

1. From the MSN Investor home page, click <u>Insight</u> on the menu bar.

2. Under Investing Basics: Step-by-Step Guides, click <u>Prepare to Invest</u>.

3. Under Step 2: Test Your Knowledge and Your Nerve, click <u>Risk Tolerance Quiz.</u>

   The <u>Financial IQ Test</u> link is also worth a detour. *See also* "Tutorial Sites" in this part.

4. After reading the brief explanation, Click <u>Quiz</u> and take the 20-question test.

5. Click Next at the bottom of the page or Results at the top. You then see two scores, one for *risk capacity* (your financial fitness) and the other for *risk tolerance* (your personal comfort level).

Based on these scores, MSN suggests an asset mix ranging from conservative to aggressive.

Quicken.com's financial health checkup

For a more detailed view of your risk capacity, take the financial health checkup at Quicken.com (www.quicken.com/saving/checkup). This questionnaire asks you how well you've met your key financial needs, such as insurance, wills, and rainy-day funds — things you need to nail down before assuming investment risk.

1. After reading the brief introduction, click Start the Checkup Now. Expect to spend 5 to 10 minutes answering the questions.

   To keep things moving, have data on hand about your assets, will, estate planning, and insurance.

2. You can answer most of the questions with pull-down menu choices or multiple-choice buttons.

   Sometimes the site asks you for amounts (as with net worth, consumer debt, and liquid new worth). Follow the links in the questions to get definitions of these terms.

3. Click Done.

   Doing so takes you to a list of seven categories — money and debt management, investments, insurance, college, taxes, retirement, and estate planning — each with colored flags indicating how well you are doing.

   Green means you're doing fine, yellow means you're OK but could improve, and red means you have a serious shortcoming that needs attention soon.

4. Click <u>Tips</u> or <u>Feedback and Tips</u> in any category to get some suggestions for improving your financial fitness.

Researching Investment Strategies

Portfolio-building is the science of combining your investment in stocks, bonds, Treasury bills, money-market funds, CDs, and other investment opportunities to produce the return you want without undue risk. Online tools such as asset allocators and screens — programs that find stocks or mutual funds meeting selected criteria — are of great help as you strategically plan your investing. **See also** "The Big Picture" for more information on the basics of getting around on the Internet.

Risk/Return calculations

MSN Investor's Asset Allocator is a good tool for studying the risk/reward balance for various asset mixes. You can also use it to link to stock and fund screens that show you how to flesh out your allocation scheme with actual securities. *See also* Part III for more on stock screens, Part VI for screening funds, and "Allocating Assets" earlier in this part for more on asset allocation.

Follow these steps:

1. At the MSN Investor home page (`www.moneycentral.msn.com/investor/home.asp`), click <u>Insight</u> on the menu bar.

2. Click <u>Step-by-Step Guides</u> in the left-hand menu.

3. Under Step 4: Build Your Investment Model, click <u>Asset Allocator</u>.

4. Click <u>Rate of Return</u>; then choose a number (between 4.5 and 11.5) from the pull-down menu next to Desired Rate of Return.

Take some time to look at the graphs on this page. They show the range of *actual* returns, over 2 years or 10 years, that you can expect for a given *desired* return. These graphs show you how volatile a high-return portfolio can be over the short term.

5. Click <u>Results</u> to get a pie chart of the suggested allocation for the rate of return you've chosen.

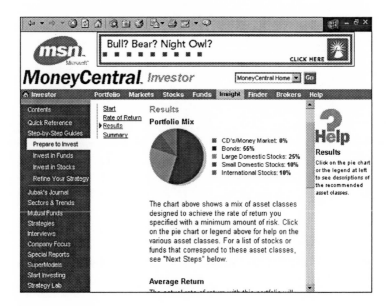

This page also tells you the variation you can expect in yearly returns over the next 10 years (Average Return), a rating of your annual risk, and the likelihood of losing money in a given year.

6. Click <u>Rate of Return</u> if you want to examine the risks of a higher or lower return.

To look for specific stocks or funds to fit the asset types in your pie chart, click the links <u>Pre-Defined Stock Searches</u> or <u>Pre-Defined Fund Searches</u>.

If you want a truly long-term look at the performance of stocks and bonds, go to the Global Financial Data site at www. globalfindata.com and click <u>Free Annual Reports</u>. To see two useful reports on the returns from stocks, bonds, and short-term investments, go to <u>Stocks, Bonds, Bills and Inflation Total Investment Returns, 1694-1996</u>, and <u>Total Returns on Stocks, Bonds, Bills and Inflation in the United States, 1871-1999</u>.

Sample portfolios

For a set of sample portfolios at various levels of risk, go to the Learning to Invest site at www.learningtoinvest.com.

1. Under Build a Portfolio, click <u>Proceed</u>.

2. Click <u>Consult the Risk Line</u> to see five theoretical asset mixes for different risk levels — Aggressive, Moderate, Middle, Conservative, and Risk-Averse.

Each shows potential one-year losses and probable multi-year rates of return.

3. Use the Back button to return to the Portfolio Building page; then click <u>Sample Portfolios</u>.

This action takes you to a Portfolio Hints page with a list of links on the right-hand side to sample portfolios of different dollar amounts and risk levels.

4. Click <u>Middle</u> under Reduced Portfolios to see specific sectors and securities that an investor with $15,000 to $30,000 might buy to create a portfolio of medium risk and return (these are theoretical lists only, not investment advice).

5. Click <u>Full Portfolio</u> to see how more than $30,000 might be invested in this risk class.

This page also has graphs showing the different asset classes and the portfolio's recent performance.

6. Click Stock Symbols.

The full names of securities are listed in the portfolio by their symbols.

7. Use the Back button to go to the Portfolio Hints page and then check out other sample portfolio links.

Comparing strategies

After you decide what risk level and asset allocation are right for you, you then need to pick specific securities that seem to be top performers in each asset class. *See also* "Allocating Assets" and "Finding Your Investment Style."

As an introduction to stock-picking strategies, visit MSN Investor (www.moneycentral.msn.com/investor/home.asp):

1. On the home page, click Insight on the menu bar.

2. Click Step-by-Step Guides and then Refine Your Strategy in the left-hand menu.

3. Click Introduction to Basic Strategies.

The link takes you to an insightful essay by Jim Jubak titled "Introduction to Basic Strategies."

MSN also shows various strategies in action. This is a good way to watch how different stock-picking criteria fare in the real world.

On the home page (www.moneycentral.msn.com/investor/home.asp), click Insight and choose one of several links from the left-hand menu:

✔ **Strategy Lab:** This page shows hypothetical portfolios created by expert investors. Check out the current total of each portfolio as well as an explanation of the expert investor's strategies.

✔ **SuperModels:** This page tracks several portfolios based on different stock-picking screens with different value and growth criteria. *See also* Part III for more on using stock screens.

✔ **Strategies:** This offers articles on market-leading stocks and the trends that push them to the top.

Setting Investment Goals

Investment planning means deciding how much money you want, when you want it, and how much you have to gain — from investment earnings and setting aside income — between now and then.

Planning for college and retirement are two major investment goals for most investors.

Using financial calculators

Using an online calculator, you can quickly see what it would take for you to, say, retire with $2 million in assets 25 years from now, or have $100,000 set aside in a college fund 10 years down the road.

You can find a full set of calculators appropriate for figuring out any type of investment goal at Financenter.com (www.financenter.com).

1. From the Financenter home page, go to ClickCalcs on the menu near the bottom of the page.

America Online users can get to the same calculators from the Personal Finance channel by going to <u>Advice & Planning</u> and scrolling to <u>Financial Calculators</u> in the right-hand menu.

2. Choose the Savings pull-down menu.

3. Select How Much, at What Rate, When?

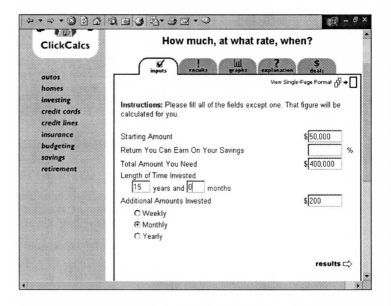

4. Fill in all the text boxes except *one* so that the calculator fills in the missing information.

5. Click Results.

    The calculator tells you the value for the field you left blank in Step 4. There are two totals: one for a tax-deferred account and one in which interest was taxable at the rates you specified.

6. Click Graphs to see how your savings grows over time.

7. Click Inputs to go back to the starting screen.

    Adjust any or all the amounts and try running the same calculation with other boxes left blank.

8. Click ClickCalcs on the bottom blue menu to go back to the main list of calculators.

Do several calculations with different rates of return to see what a difference a few percentage points can make in long-term investing. **See also** "Planning for college: Determining total cost" and "Planning for retirement: Determining yearly costs" for other specific calculators you can use at the Financenter site.

Planning for college: Determining total cost

If you want some help figuring out the full amount that it will cost to send a child to college, take a look at Charles Schwab's "College Saver," one of the planning features at the broker's home page, www.schwab.com.

Follow these steps to get a clearer picture of college costs and what you must do to meet them:

1. At the Schwab home page, access the Get Started With pull-down menu, select College Planning, and then click Go.

2. Fill in the boxes on the right for each child — name, age, and whether the child will attend a public or private college.

3. Click Continue to open a Define Your Goal window, with an estimated cost figure (which you can change) and assumptions about when the child will attend and for how long.

    You can change these assumptions by clicking Change Assumptions.

4. When you're ready to go ahead, click Continue.

    The Develop a Plan window opens, with assumptions about your future savings and your rate of return.

    You can change any figure and re-run the calculations by clicking Calculate New Savings Goal or Calculate New Monthly Payment.

5. Click Continue to see some questions about the type of account you might want to set up.

   You can call up more windows to learn more about Schwab's college-saving plans or to change your risk tolerance level (from "aggressive" to "conservative," for instance) and see different plans.

Planning for college: Determining yearly costs

Bloomberg.com (`www.bloomberg.com`) has a college-cost calculator that fits the way tuition is actually paid — not in one lump sum, but over several years.

1. On the Bloomberg home page, click the Tools icon.

2. Under Calculators, click <u>Education Cost Calculator</u> and fill in the boxes.

3. Click Calculate after filling in the boxes (you have to make your own estimate of the annual cost) to see the required savings plan.

   Note: The calculator uses a before-tax return and asks for your tax rate. Be sure the tax rate figure reflects state as well as federal taxes.

By changing the savings plan or payout frequency, you can change the amount you need to save. More frequent savings installments (weekly instead of yearly, for instance), lower the total, as do more frequent tuition payments (quarterly, say, instead of annually).

Planning for retirement

Financenter.com has a comprehensive retirement worksheet, covering financial issues ranging from Social Security to post-retirement inflation and tax rates.

The worksheet also has spaces for current balances, contributions, and rates of returns for all types of retirement savings accounts, tax-deferred and otherwise. Even if you only do part of it, you still get answers to some key questions, such as your future Social Security benefits. Here's how:

1. At the Financenter home page (`www.financenter.com`), click ClickCalcs.

2. Go to the Retirement pull-down menu and choose Am I Saving Enough? What Can I Change?

3. Fill out the Personal Information section, which includes age, income, tax rates, and other basic data for you and your spouse.

4. Scroll down to the section called Monthly Living Expenses when Retired.

   You can either use the suggested amounts or plug in your own.

5. Go to the bottom of the form, choose How Much Will Social Security Provide? and then click Results.

6. After examining a graph estimating how much you and your spouse will receive, click Explanation to learn how the calculator arrived at this forecast.

7. Click Inputs to return to the worksheet. Try running another calculation.

8. Choose the question, How Much Can I Invest before Taxes Each Year?, and click Graphs.

   You see a list of amounts you may be able to put in tax-deferred accounts such as Keoghs, IRAs, and SIMPLEs, based on your income.

9. To measure your progress toward your retirement goals, you need to fill out the rest of the worksheet, including data on expected pensions (if any) and your savings and tax-deferred accounts.

   You're asked to predict a rate of return for accounts both before and after retirement. As a rule, you would shift into less risky investments as you grow older, so the rate of return should fall as well (from 10 percent before to 6 percent after, for example).

10. At the bottom of the worksheet, choose Am I Saving Enough? What Should I Change? and then click Results.

    The site shows you whether you're saving enough and earning enough on your investments.

11. Click Graphs to see your future income-expense pattern in chart form.

12. Click Inputs and try re-running the calculations with different numbers, such as higher rates of return or post-retirement expenses.

Financenter has a separate sheet for calculating post-retirement living expenses. From the Retirement pull-down menu, choose What Will My Expenses Be After I Retire?

Bloomberg.com gives you a calculator just for your 401(k), using employee and employer contributions to come up with future projections of the account's value.

1. Go to www.bloomberg.com and click Tools in the menu bar.

2. Click <u>401k Calculator</u> in the Calculators list.

3. Try the <u>Savings Calculator</u> link on that list if your question is a simple one: What will it take for me to retire a millionaire?

Comparing IRAs

For investors who can qualify for both regular and Roth IRAs, the task of comparing the two as investment vehicles can be daunting. Financenter has a calculator that compares regular and Roth IRAs as investment vehicles.

1. From www.financenter.com, go to ClickCalcs.

2. Choose one of the questions under the heading Roth IRA.

Any of these questions leads to a worksheet that you can fill out to calculate answers to one of the questions listed at the bottom.

Tutorial Sites and Tools

Several financial Web sites, such as MSN Investor, stand out as good places to learn about investing — not just a place to collect data and news.

From the MSN Investor home page, follow the <u>Insight</u> link to see tutorials. <u>Quick Reference</u> and <u>Step-by-Step Guides</u> are the best links for beginners or investors who want to refresh their knowledge.

Here are some other sites that make a serious effort to educate:

- ✔ **The Motley Fool.** This pioneer of online stock analysis is still mostly focused on stocks, but its "Fool's School" covers all aspects of investing. Go to www.fool.com/School.htm.

- ✔ **SmartMoney University.** The personal-finance magazine's online branch has a complete roster of investing tutorials. Go to www.university.smartmoney.com and check out the list under Departments. The <u>Investing 101</u> link is a good starting point for beginners.

- ✔ **Vanguard University.** The Vanguard Group, a leading mutual fund family, has a Web site packed with education that you can apply to all types of investing. From the home page at www.vanguard.com, click the Education, Planning & Advice tab and then click University.

Part II

Understanding Stock Quotes and Charts

A wealth of stock data is available through the Internet, starting with quotes — a display of prices along with other current information — and charts of price and volume action. Together, they give you a portrait of a stock in number and picture form. You can use this data to look for patterns that signal opportunities to buy and sell. This part tells you where to find these online resources and how to use them.

In this part . . .

After-Hours Quotes

The action ends in the main U.S. stock markets at 4 p.m. eastern time, but trading continues for many stocks well after that in electronic communication networks (ECNs). These give buyers and sellers a way to trade directly, without going through middlemen such as NASDAQ dealers or stock exchange specialists.

No single entity records prices at all the ECNs, so finding the best price at any given time isn't easy. But with after-hours trading becoming more popular, ECNs have started to post their prices.

✔ Island ECN (www.island.com) posts live trades in real-time on its BookViewer. You can see the last recorded sale and a list of recent buy and sell orders.

✔ MarketXT (www.marketxt.com) lists its current most active stocks. To see all the stocks traded on this system, click the Go button below the most-active list.

Basic Quote Data

A basic quote includes the price of a stock, usually with additional data such as trading volume, the change in price from the previous day's close, and the day's highs and lows. To call up a basic quote, you can go to an online financial site, such as MSN Investor, Yahoo! Finance, Quicken.com, or AOL Finance. All these sites have similar procedures for getting this information.

See also "The Big Picture" for more information on the basics of getting around on the Internet.

To call up a basic quote:

1. Go to the financial site you want. Some financial sites that you may want to visit include:

   • MSN Investor (www.moneycentral.msn.com/investor)

   • Yahoo! Finance (www.finance.yahoo.com)

   • Quicken.com (www.quicken.com/investments)

   • AOL Finance (the Personal Finance channel)

2. On the financial site home page, look for a box labeled Get Quotes, or something similar, and then click this box.

3. Type the *trading symbol* in the appropriate field.

   See also "Trading Symbols" in this part for more on the letter codes used to identify stocks.

4. Click the adjoining command button — Get Quotes or something similar.

Quoted price

A stock quote highlights the *quoted price*, the price at which the stock was sold on its last trade. That number is usually the first or most prominent number in online quotes.

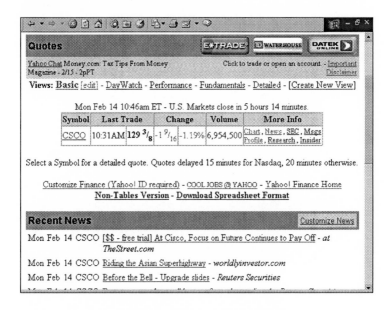

A basic quote also includes the change from the previous day's *closing price*. In this figure, that value is expressed in *points* (dollars per share) and a percentage.

Daily price range

At most financial sites, you can also check out the daily price range for a stock. For example, after calling up a basic quote at Yahoo!, click the DayWatch link, and you see three additional items of data:

✔ Average volume

✔ Opening price

✔ Day's price range

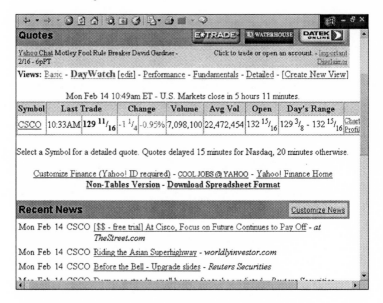

The price figures tell you whether the stock is trading near its high or low for the day. That's a clue as to whether it's headed up or down in value. To confirm whether the stock is headed up or down (and whether the volume reinforces that trend), you need to call up a chart and a real-time quote. *See also* "Charting" and "Real-time Quotes" in this part for more on both topics.

Trade times (and quote delays)

The trade time shown in basic quotes is when the latest sale was recorded (in eastern time). Prices are delayed at least 20 minutes for shares listed on the New York Stock Exchange and American Stock Exchange, and at least 15 minutes for NASDAQ listings. This delay isn't a problem when you want a rough idea of where a stock is headed. But you must have real-time prices before you actually buy or sell a stock. *See also* "Real-time Quotes."

Quote delays don't matter after exchanges have closed and if you're not interested in after-hours trading. The stock market closes at 4:00 p.m. eastern time, so if you're looking at a NASDAQ stock much after 4:15 p.m. eastern time, you're probably looking at the true closing price. Ditto for NYSE stocks after 4:20 p.m.

Daily and average volume

The *Volume* figure you see in a basic quote simply counts how many shares of the stock have changed hands so far in the trading day. Like price, it measures the strength of demand for a stock or the eagerness of holders to sell.

How heavy is the volume? That depends on how many shares are typically traded each day. The DayWatch quote at Yahoo! gives you a useful measuring stick in its Average Volume figure, which is based on daily trading totals from the past three months.

In looking for volume moves, remember that the average figure is for a *whole* trading session. A stock can be trading heavily and still seem below average early in the day.

Bid and ask prices

At some financial sites, such as MSN Investor, a basic quote can include:

- **Bid price:** The highest price that buyers will pay for a stock.

- **Ask price:** The lowest price (or "offer") that sellers will accept.

The bid and ask prices together are called a *quotation*.

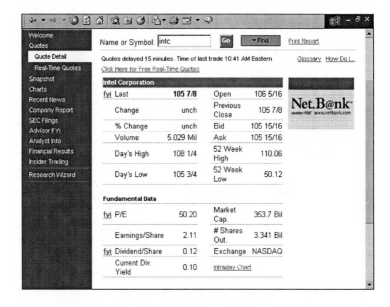

If the quote is for a NASDAQ stock, you see the Bid and Ask prices in the second column of the quote table (the New York Stock Exchange does not give bid and ask data on delayed quotes).

The Ask price is what you usually would pay to buy a stock. If you're actually trading, you must get a *real-time* quote first from your online brokerage, because a lot can happen during the 15 to 20 minute lag-time of delayed quotes. *See also* "Real-time Quotes."

Yearly price range

Basic quotes from MSN Investor and other financial sites include a range of prices from the past 52-week period. This range tells you whether a stock is at or near a new high or low, though you need a chart to get a clearer picture of its price trend.

Earnings per share (EPS)

EPS refers to *earnings per share.* This is a company's *net income* divided by the number of *shares outstanding.* Usually, the EPS given in a stock quote refers to earnings per share for the latest four quarters. In an annual report, it's based on a company's earnings for a fiscal year (not necessarily the latest four quarters). In a quarterly report, it signifies just the latest quarter's earnings (usually compared to the EPS for the corresponding quarter in the prior fiscal year).

Price/Earnings (P/E) ratio

Divide the quoted price by the past four quarters' EPS (*see also* "Earnings per Share"), and you get the much-watched price/earnings (P/E) ratio.

The P/E ratio is crucial because it compares a stock's price to the company's central measure of value, its profit. A high P/E usually means investors expect profit to rise. A lower P/E means they expect profit to stay flat or fall. So fast growth and very high P/Es tend to go hand-in-hand. Some of the most hotly-traded stocks don't have earnings (or P/Es) at all, and investors flock to these stocks because they expect high profits sometime in the future.

You need to interpret P/E ratios in context. A high-P/E company may still be a bargain if it's lower than that of companies in the same industry that are growing just as fast or faster. *See also* Part III for more on comparing company ratios to industries and the general market.

Market capitalization

Some basic quotes show a number labeled "market capitalization" or "market cap." You can see it, for instance, at MSN Investor listed under Fundamental Data in a stock quote.

Market capitalization is the number of shares outstanding multiplied by the current stock price. Comparing market cap to a company's total annual (not per-share) revenue or earnings is one way to measure how "pricey" a stock may be; in this way, it's something like the P/E ratio.

Market cap is also used to classify stocks and mutual fund portfolios. Experts set different boundaries:

✔ **Small-cap** stocks are usually those worth $1 billion or less (issues under $100 million sometimes are put in a separate *micro-cap* category).

✔ **Mid-cap** stocks are usually worth up to $5 billion or so.

✔ **Large-cap** stocks include everything above that.

See also Part VIII, "Mutual Funds," for more on the small-cap and large-cap labels in classifying funds.

Shares outstanding

The number of shares that have been issued by the company, including those *not* available to the investing public, are called *shares outstanding.* Changes in this total can influence earnings per share comparisons. If a company's profits rise 20 percent in a year and its shares outstanding do the same, its EPS will not change. Share *buybacks,* in which a company reduces shares outstanding by buying them up, can have the opposite effect.

The number of shares available for public trading is called the *float.* When the float is small and trading is heavy, prices can be highly volatile.

Dividends and yield

If a stock pays *dividends* to shareholders, a basic quote often gives the annual payout per share, based on the latest dividend paid or declared. The *yield* is this annual rate (annual payout per share) divided by the stock price.

Dividend payments are limited to those who own the stock on a *date of record.* For example, on March 1, a company might declare a dividend to be paid on April 1 to anyone holding stock on March 15. March 15 is the date of record. After that, the stock trades *ex-dividend* — that is, those who buy shares in that period don't get the dividend.

If you're buying a stock and wondering whether you miss out on the next dividend, click the Detailed link above a Yahoo! quote (or choose Detailed from the pull-down quote menu) and check the date in the Ex-Div box.

Charting

Online charts all serve the same purpose — to put a stock's daily numbers (which appear in a basic quote) in the context of a stock's history. Charts show past trends in price and volume and give clues to a stock's possible moves in the future.

Yahoo! charts are on the simple side, but they're fast-loading, easy to adjust, and easy to read. They also come with a full stock quote, and you can call up more than one chart at a time.

Call up a Yahoo! chart by following these steps:

1. At the Yahoo! Finance home page (`quote.yahoo.com`), type one or more ticker symbols in the field next to the Get Quotes button.

2. Select Chart from the pull-down menu to the right.

3. Click Get Quotes. A price/volume chart appears along with the latest price and other quote data.

If you already called up a basic quote at Yahoo!, you can click the Chart link in the More Info box to see the chart for the quote. Or, in a detailed Yahoo! quote, click 1 Year in the list of links that appears under the small chart to call up a one-year chart.

The resulting screen shows two charts with the following information:

- ✓ A large chart with quote data at the top and lists of links at the bottom

- ✓ Prices for the past year, adjusted for splits and dividends, up to the previous day's close

- ✓ A second chart below the price chart, that shows trading volume

Changing a chart's time frame

Yahoo! charts can show prices and volume over several different periods, from one day to more than five years (if the stock has been around that long). Use the links listed after Big at the bottom of the screen to choose a time-frame.

Some differences appear in the way data is displayed in each Big chart:

- ✔ **1 day:** Traces prices to the latest price (with the normal quote delay) in the trading day. A dotted red line shows the previous day's close, and volume is shown on a minute-by-minute scale.

- ✔ **5 day:** Shows a price chart of the current trading day and the four previous days. Here you can see whether a stock has "gapped" up or down — opened sharply above or below the previous day's close.

- ✔ **3 month:** Shows a bar chart (instead of a line chart) that displays prices. Each bar shows the high-low range for the day. A tick pointing left shows the opening price, and a tick pointing right shows the close. Compare these bars to the daily volume graph, just below it, to see if any sharp price moves have been accompanied by heavy trading.

- ✔ **2 year, 5 year,** and **max:** Show longer-term price and volume trends. The max chart shows stocks back to their initial public offerings or to 1970, whichever is later.

Showing trends with moving averages

Moving averages tune out the daily peaks and valleys of a stock price and show its longer-term direction. They also give you a benchmark for assessing the stock's next move. If a stock's current price crosses (or "breaks through") a long-term moving average, for instance, it may be ending one long-term trend and starting a new one.

A moving average is calculated from the prices for certain periods, such as 50 days or 200 days, prior to each time interval on the chart. A 50-day moving average, for instance, is the average each day of the prior 50 days of closing prices. A moving average can be based on weeks, days, hours, or minutes.

To see a moving average online:

1. Go to a one-year chart at Yahoo! Finance.

2. Click the Moving Avg link.

You see two relatively smooth lines, showing 50-day and 200-day moving averages.

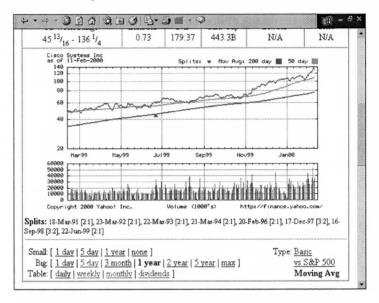

Check out the moving averages for different stocks to see whether you can find some that have cut through upward or downward moving-average trends and reversed course. **See also** Part VI for more on using trend-spotting tools such as moving averages.

Comparing a stock against the market

To measure a stock's performance against the market as a whole, call up any Big Yahoo! chart for a three-month period or longer and click the vs S&P 500 link. This link compares a stock's performance to the performance of the Standard & Poor's 500, an index of the largest U.S. stocks and the most common gauge of the general market.

Remember: A red line represents the S&P 500's performance; a blue line, the stock's. If the stock line ends the period above the red index line, the stock has beaten the market as measured by the S&P 500.

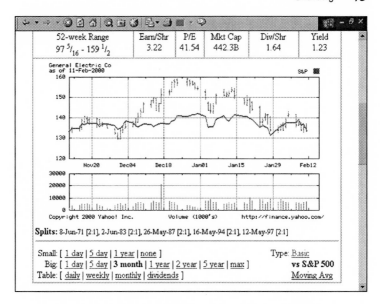

52-week Range	Earn/Shr	P/E	Mkt Cap	Div/Shr	Yield
97 5/16 - 159 1/2	3.22	41.54	442.3B	1.64	1.23

Another number for measuring performance against the market is the *relative strength* number calculated by some stock data services. It's based on a scale of 1 to 99, with the highest numbers representing the strongest performance against a market index, normally the S&P 500. You can find the relative strength value in some enhanced quotes sites. **See also** "Enhanced Quotes."

Comparing a stock with competitors

If you want to compare a stock to some competitors, try the charts at Quicken.com. Here you can compare stocks to indexes, moving averages, or other stocks over periods from one day to five years.

1. Go to Quicken.com's investor home page at www.quicken.com/investments.

2. Enter a ticker symbol in the Quotes and Research box and choose the Chart option.

3. Click Go.

   You see a price and volume chart for your stock, with menus just above the upper (price) chart.

   • The menu on the left lets you choose time periods from less than a day to five years.

- The menu on the right gives you a choice between display-ing closing prices or return on $10,000 invested in the stock (the Growth of $10K option).

4. Select closing prices from the menu on the right.

5. To add stocks for comparison, type other trading symbols (separated by spaces) in the Symbol(s) box.

6. Click Go.

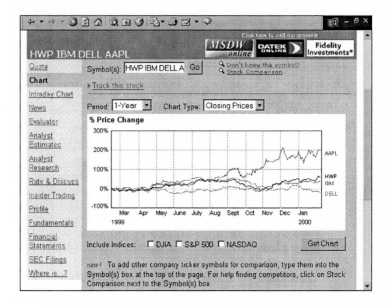

The chart displays a line for each stock, all starting from the same point on the left. Instead of showing actual closing prices, the lines show the percentage gain or loss for each stock for the period chosen.

7. To add the performance of an index, check the appropriate check box below the chart and click Get Chart.

You can choose three indexes — Dow Jones Industrial Average, NASDAQ Composite, and S&P 500 — but that may make the chart difficult to read.

8. If you want, pick a new time frame from the Period pull-down menu.

Try 3-Year for a longer-term chart, which gives you a different picture of these stocks' performance relative to one another.

If you want to find out just who a company's main rivals are, click the <u>Compare Stock to Competitors</u> link just above any Quicken.com chart. You then see a list of companies in the same industry as the stock you're tracking. Check any of them you want to chart; then click Go. You can also add symbols here for stocks not included in Quicken's comparison.

Comparing a stock to an industry-group index

To measure a stock against an industry-group index, you can also try the charts at MSN Investor. Follow these steps:

1. Go to the MSN Investor home page (moneycentral.msn.com/investor).

2. Type a symbol in the box at the upper left-hand corner.

3. Choose Chart from the pull-down menu just to the right.

4. Click Go.

5. On the right-hand side of the chart, click the Industry Avg box.

    A second line appears on the price chart. If you need to find a symbol or see a list of indexes, click the Find button.

6. Place the cursor on the line to find the name of the index and get its closing price on any given day.

    You can also get prices in this way for the stock. If you click any point in the chart, you can see the high, low, close, and volume for that day.

As with Quicken.com charts, you can add stocks as well as indexes to the charts at MSN. Just type symbols in the Compare With box and click Add. **See also** "Interactive Charting" for more MSN Investor features.

Custom Charting

Some sites give you charting tools that go well beyond simple comparisons and moving averages. These custom charts enable you to use a wide range of technical indicators to analyze your stocks.

Two of the best charts are at MSN Investor and ASK Research.

Custom charting with MSN Investor

To use the MSN charting tools:

1. Go to moneycentral.msn.com/investor.

2. Type a symbol in the top left-hand box.

3. Choose Chart from the pull-down menu just to the right.

4. Click Go.

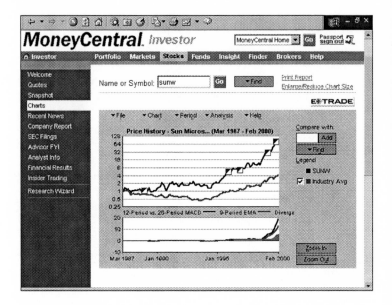

A price chart with several menu commands appears. Check out the following menus:

- The File menu has commands for importing and exporting data.

- The Chart menu enables you to change the chart type and display settings to show investment return or price performance over various time periods.

- The Period menu enables you to choose a time frame ranging from less than a day to All Dates (as far back as 1970). You can also specify a date range.

- The Analysis menu lets you add indexes, moving averages, and price-range indicators. Also, you can get a list of price and volume indicators, such as on-balance volume, and moving average convergence-divergence (MACD). **See also** Part VI for more on these indicators.

  You can also display this information in a second chart below the main price graph.

- The Help menu offers a glossary of technical charting terms.

Custom charting with ASK Research

To build charts at ASK Research:

1. Go to the home page (`www.askresearch.com`).

2. Click either Daily Charts or Intraday Charts, depending on the time period you want to use.

   A screen appears with a table of pull-down menus for display settings, overlays, and various indicators of price/volume patterns. You can click one of the links under Indicator Chart Settings to get to a definition.

3. Click the Instructions link for more information.

4. After you make your choices, click the Create Charts button.

Customizing Quotes

Yahoo! enables you to customize the type of information you receive in quotes. You can choose from the following types of quotes, all of which have links to company research in their More Info box:

✔ **Basic:** Latest price, volume, and change from the previous close.

✔ **DayWatch:** The basic quote plus average daily volume and the day's price range.

✔ **Performance:** A quote format for portfolio tracking, with data on shares owned, purchase price, and gain or loss on the holdings.

✔ **Fundamentals:** The latest price along with market cap, earnings per share, and P/E ratio.

✔ **Detailed:** All the information in Basic, DayWatch, and Fundamentals, along with bid and ask prices, dividend data, and a small chart.

You choose any of these types of quotes from the links that appear just above a quote grid; four of them (excluding Performance) also appear in the pull-down menu next to the Get Quotes button.

If you're a registered user at Yahoo!, you can use two links for additional customization:

✔ **Customizing a setting:** After you call up a quote, click any of the View links (such as Basic or DayWatch); then click the Edit link to change the data mix in that view.

    ✔ **Creating a new setting:** Click the <u>Create New View</u> link to set
      up a quote you can label yourself.

Either link takes you to a screen that lets you construct a new view.
The screen shown here is for customizing a Basic quote:

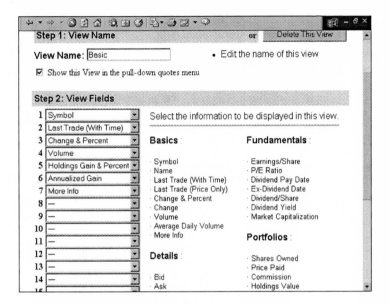

1. In Step 1, change the view name, label the new view you're
   creating, or leave the name the same.

2. In Step 2, use the pull-down menus that appear in a column on
   the left to choose the data that you want to appear in your
   custom view.

   All the available types of data are listed on the right.

3. After you're done, click the Accept Changes button at the
   bottom of the page.

See also Part X.

Enhanced Quote Data

Plenty of online sites give you basic quote features — price and
volume, P/E, market cap, highs and lows, dividends, and so forth.
See also "Basic Quote Data" in this part.

A few online sites include types of data that aren't so common.
Here are some enhanced quote features and where to find them.

Beta and volatility

Stocks vary in the way they reflect the movement of the market in general. Some are more volatile, others less so.

Beta is a measurement of volatility. Stocks are rated in a scale in which 1.0 indicates price action no more or less volatile than the market.

- ✔ A beta below 1.0 means less volatility, which may make a stock more suitable for a conservative investor.

- ✔ A beta above 1.0 means the stock tends to hit higher highs and lower lows than the broad indexes. Its rewards and risks tend to be greater as well.

America Online's basic quote includes the beta for many stocks. AOL subscribers can call up a quote by following these steps:

1. At the AOL welcome page (the first page you see after logging in), click AOL Channels.

2. Click Personal Finance.

3. Type a stock symbol in the box labeled Enter Ticker Symbol.

4. Click Get Quote.

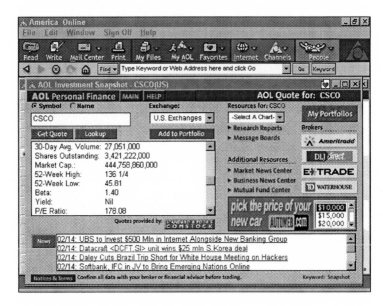

5. Scroll down the quote box to find the beta number.

6. To check the beta of another stock, type a symbol in the top left box and click Get Quote.

To get a better idea of how low-beta and high-beta stocks compare, try calling up charts, using the Resources For pull-down menu. You may notice that low-beta stocks aren't necessarily safe — some trail far behind market averages.

You can also find a beta number at the Bloomberg Web site (www.bloomberg.com). *See also* "Relative P/E and yield" and "Earning growth comparisons" in this part for other Bloomberg quote features.

Relative strength

From a stock's relative strength (RS) number, you can see how well it is doing compared to the rest of the market.

✔ A number above 50 (on a 1-to-99 scale) means it has beaten the averages for the specified period. A number below 50 means it has lagged.

✔ A number above 90 puts it in an elite group of leaders.

The 123Jump Web site shows a stock's relative strength not just for one time frame but for three — three months, six months, and one year. The time frames can tell you something about a stock's consistency and whether it may be losing ground. (That may be happening if a stock's three-month RS is much lower than the one-year figure.)

To use 123Jump's detailed quotes:

1. Go to www.123jump.com.

2. Type a stock symbol in the left-hand box at the top of the page.

3. Select Detailed Quote from the box to the right.

4. Click Jump.

A table of data appears.

Last	Change	% Change	Day Low	Day High	Volume	Prev Volume
115 $^{13}/_{16}$	$^7/_{16}$	0.38 %	114 $^1/_2$	116 $^3/_8$	1,822,000	4,961,500
Time	Last Size	# Trades	Bid	Ask	% Volume Chg	Average Volume
11:44	100	1429	N/A	N/A	-70.29%	6,131,856
14d MA	50d MA	200d MA	Open	Prev Close	Outst Shr(000)	Market Cap(000)
115.76	113.33	115.84	116	115 $^3/_8$	1,802,604	207,299,460
3m RS	6m RS	1yr RS	Yr Low	Yr High	Div/Shr	Earn/Shr
65	40	62	80 $^7/_8$	139 $^3/_{16}$	0.48	4.12
3m Return	6m Return	1yr Return	Yr Low on	Yr High on	Yield	P/E
18.88%	-6.49%	29.61%	04/20/99	07/13/99	0.41%	28.11

IBM INTL BUSINESS MACH (More News)

02/14-10:53	MN	PERLE SYSTEMS LTD - Signs Distribution Agreement
02/14-10:35	MT	EXTENDED SYSTEMS: Extended Systems releases XTNDConnect PC
02/14-10:15	TW	Microsoft Is Finally Opening Windows 2000
02/14-10:15	PR	Cognos(R) Partner Success Story: Wine.com Toasts Successful
02/14-10:07	PR	Computer Network Technology Appoints Vice President Enterprise
02/14-10:00	BW	IdeaScope Joins Lighthouse Global Network
02/14-09:58	BW	Network Solutions Seeks Competitive Edge Through First
02/14-09:35	PR	Luminant Announces Earnings Release Date
02/14-09:33	BW	OSA Announces NETDEPLOY GLOBAL Software Management; Active

5. In the table of data, look for *3m RS, 6m RS,* and *1yr RS.*

Right below these, you find total return figures for the three periods. Right above, you find moving averages of the stock's price for 14 days, 50 days, and 200 days.

123Jump offers one of the most data-rich quotes around. Among other things, it's a good place to check for changes from average volume. Note the % Volume Chg number. **See also** Part VI for more on interpreting volume and price patterns.

Relative P/E and yield

Another way of comparing a stock to the market is to look at its Price/Earnings (P/E) ratio and dividend yield in relation to those figures for stocks in general. Relative P/E divides the P/E of a particular stock by the combined P/E ratio of all the stocks in a market index such as the S&P 500.

Bloomberg.com gives you this figure, as well as a similar calculation for dividend yield. To find a stock's relative P/E:

1. Go to the Bloomberg.com home page at www.bloomberg.com.

2. Type a symbol under Stock Quotes.

3. Click Go.

A basic quote appears.

4. From the menu on the right, choose Detailed Quote.

5. Click Go.

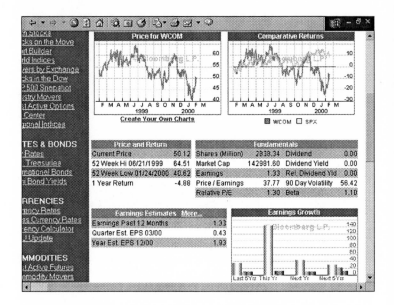

You find relative P/E and relative dividend yield in the Fundamentals section, just below the small charts.

Earnings growth comparisons

Bloomberg's detailed quotes also give you a look, in graphic form, at a company's profit growth compared to its industry and the market. On the Detailed Quote screen you call up for relative P/E and relative yield (*see also* "Relative P/E and Yield"), look at a chart labeled Earnings Growth.

Bar graphs show how fast the earnings for this stock, the S&P 500, and the stock's industry group have grown in the last year and over the past five years.

Historical Quotes

If you want to know exactly what a stock sold for on a particular date (as well as its high, low, and volume), you can pull up historical quotes at various sites.

At Yahoo!, you can get historical quotes by first calling up a chart on a stock (*see also* "Charting") and then following these steps:

1. Click one of the links on the Table list below the charts.

- The Daily option gives you a table of daily highs, lows, closes, and volume going back three months.

- The Weekly option gives you a year's worth of such data, tallied by week.

- The Monthly option goes back two years.

2. Use the pull-down menus, boxes, and buttons at the top of the chart to alter each of these tables to change the time period, the interval (days, weeks, or months), or the stock.

A daily chart, for instance, can be extended to six months by setting the Start Date fields back three months.

3. After you change any settings, click the Get Historical Data button to see the new chart.

These charts show both actual prices and prices adjusted for subsequent splits. This makes it easy to calculate how much a stock has actually grown in value (and to avoid mistakes in figuring your capital gains). If a stock has split two-for-one — that is, the number of shares was doubled and the per-share price was cut in half — the earlier split-adjusted price is half the actual price. Splits are also noted in the table on the dates when they occur. *See also* "split" in the Glossary.

Real-time Quotes

Some financial Web sites give you the option of calling up real-time stock quotes. (When making any online trades, of course, you would get these quotes at your broker's site.)

Real-time quotes lack some of the data of delayed quotes, and they can require a log-in that can make access a bit slower. But they're current, and they're free.

After you get through the initial registration for a site, you can bring up real-time quotes without a separate log-in. *See also* Appendix A, "Customizing Financial Portals," for more on the registration process.

To get a real-time quote for MSN Investor:

1. From the MSN Investor home page, click Stocks on the menu bar.

2. Click Quotes in the left-hand menu.

3. Click Real-Time Quotes in the left-hand menu.

4. Type a trading symbol in the box next to Name or Symbol.

   Typing a company name takes you to a symbol-search program.

5. Click Go.

The quote gives you the usual basic data such as latest price, change from the previous close, bid and ask prices, and the open, close, high, and low for the day.

The quote also has two items of useful data if you want to get a sense of the stock's upward or downward momentum.

✔ The Tick arrow shows whether the price of the last sale was above, below, or equal to the last.

✔ The Bid/Ask Size shows how many shares are being offered at the current Ask price, compared to the number of shares wanted at the current Bid price. **See also** Part V for the importance of ticks in short selling.

You can use the Refresh button on your browser to call up a new quote for this stock. Real-time quotes are updated with each new trade, which can be every few seconds to every few minutes, depending on the activity in the stock.

Ticker Symbols

Don't know the ticker symbol for a stock? Most financial sites have a symbol-search link conveniently near the commands you use to call up quotes or charts.

✔ At Yahoo! Finance, click <u>Symbol Lookup</u> just to the right of the pull-down quotes menu.

✔ At Quicken.com, you can click the <u>Don't Know the Symbol?</u> link.

✔ At MSN Investor, look up the symbol by clicking Stocks on the horizontal menu bar and then clicking the Find button just below.

Stocks with tickers of four or more letters are traded on NASDAQ. Those with three letters or fewer are on the New York or American (AMEX) exchanges. Five-letter symbols ending in "X" signify mutual funds.

Company Research and News

This part tells how to find essential company data, such as corporate overviews and financial results, on the Internet. It describes the information you can find through financial home pages, Web searches, and online news archives.

In this part . . .

Company Profiles

At Internet financial sites, you can usually find one-page company profiles that contain essential information, such as product lines, stock performance, and financial highlights.

Here are some sites where you can find corporate snapshots. First, call up a quote at the home page and then use the link specified in the following table.

Host Site	URL	Click this Link
123Jump	www.123jump.com	Company Profile, then Jump
Bloomberg	www.bloomberg.com	Company Profile
CNET	investor.cnet.com	Profile
Hoover's	www.hoovers.com	Go
MSN	investor.msn.com	Company Report
Netscape	personalfinance.netscape.com	Profile
Quicken	www.quicken.com	Company Profile
Stockpoint	www.stockpoint.com	Company Profile
Yahoo!	quote.yahoo.com	Profile

Most of the company snapshots in the preceding minitable contain similar information. Here's what you find at one in particular, Yahoo! Finance:

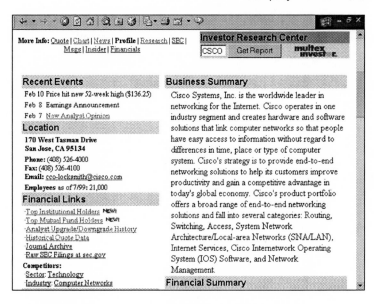

✔ **Research:** This link takes you to a summary of analysts' ratings and earnings estimates. *See also* "Tracking Financial Analysts" in this part.

✔ **SEC:** This link leads to excerpts from the latest quarterly report (10-Q) filed with the Securities and Exchange Commission. *See also* "SEC Filings" in this part.

✔ **Msgs:** Takes you to a message board devoted to this stock.

✔ **Insider:** Click here for a report on buying and selling by people with the closest knowledge of the company.

✔ **Financials:** Links you to the most recent balance sheet, income statement, and cash flow statement for the stock.

✔ **Business Summary** and **Financial Summary:** These sections describe the company's business and sum up its sales and earnings performance. Below this is a list of top officers with their compensation (when figures are available).

✔ **Top Institutional Holders** and **Top Mutual Fund Holders:** Links to a page showing you the big *institutions* whose buying and selling power helps move the stock price. *Net Inst. Buying* at the bottom of this column tells whether they've recently been mainly buyers or sellers. Just above that is a summary of ownership by institutions and *insiders.*

Scroll down the Profile page to find a data table that provides a quick overview of the company's finances and market performance.

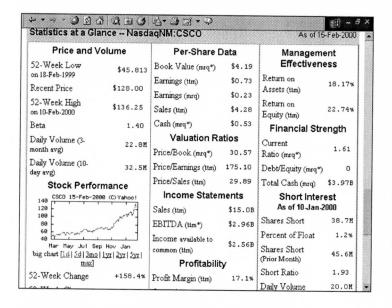

Specifically, look for the following information:

- ✔ **Float:** *Float* is the number of shares actually available for trading by the public. The bigger the float, generally, the lower a stock's volatility.

- ✔ **Short interest:** *Short interest* shows what percent of the float consists of shares that have been borrowed and sold in the hope that they can be repurchased later at a lower price. The larger this number, the greater the *bearish* sentiment — expectation of a fall in price — toward the stock.

See also "Financial Analysis" for similar information.

Financial Analysis

For a closer look at sales, profit, book value, stock performance, and other measures of financial performance, find the link labeled <u>Financials</u> or something similar at the company snapshot page of most investor sites.

Financial information from Market Guide

One of the best sites for getting in-depth financial information about a company is Market Guide.

1. Go to www.marketguide.com.

2. Enter a stock symbol in the box at the upper left of the screen.

3. Click Go.

This brings you to a Snapshot Report. The Key Ratios and Statistics table shows both stock action and the underlying financial performance of a company.

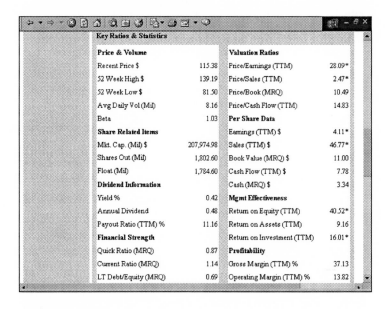

Key Ratios & Statistics			
Price & Volume		**Valuation Ratios**	
Recent Price $	115.38	Price/Earnings (TTM)	28.09*
52 Week High $	139.19	Price/Sales (TTM)	2.47*
52 Week Low $	81.50	Price/Book (MRQ)	10.49
Avg Daily Vol (Mil)	8.16	Price/Cash Flow (TTM)	14.83
Beta	1.03	**Per Share Data**	
Share Related Items		Earnings (TTM) $	4.11*
Mkt. Cap. (Mil) $	207,974.98	Sales (TTM) $	46.77*
Shares Out (Mil)	1,802.60	Book Value (MRQ) $	11.00
Float (Mil)	1,784.60	Cash Flow (TTM) $	7.78
Dividend Information		Cash (MRQ) $	3.34
Yield %	0.42	**Mgmt Effectiveness**	
Annual Dividend	0.48	Return on Equity (TTM)	40.52*
Payout Ratio (TTM) %	11.16	Return on Assets (TTM)	9.16
Financial Strength		Return on Investment (TTM)	16.01*
Quick Ratio (MRQ)	0.87	**Profitability**	
Current Ratio (MRQ)	1.14	Gross Margin (TTM) %	37.13
LT Debt/Equity (MRQ)	0.69	Operating Margin (TTM) %	13.82

The following lists the information you can get from a Key Ratios and Statistics table:

✔ Share-Related Items

- Mkt. Cap: How much a company is worth overall on the stock market

- Shares Out: The number of total shares outstanding

- Float: The number of total shares outstanding that are available for public trading

✔ Financial Strength

- Quick Ratio: How readily a company could pay short-term debt out of its cash and other liquid assets.

- Current Ratio: Short-term assets (receivables, cash, inventory) divided by short-term debt.

- LT Debt/Equity: Long-term debts (due in a year or more) as a share of the company's net worth.

✔ Valuation Ratios

- Price/Earnings: The stock-market value of a company compared to its profits

- Price/Sales: The stock-market value of a company compared to its revenue

- Price/Book: The stock-market value of a company compared to its Book Value, a measure of its net assets

- Price/Cash Flow: The stock-market value of a company compared to its cash profits (before writeoffs such as depreciation)

Other headings show various aspects of the company's profit and sales performance:

✔ Per Share Data: Earnings, sales, book value (net worth), cash flow, and cash, all divided by the number of shares outstanding.

✔ Management Effectiveness: Three ways of describing profit as a return on capital.

✔ Profitability: Three levels of profit — gross margin, operating margin, and profit margin (also known as net income or "the bottom line.")

For detailed explanations of these financial terms, use the link at the top of the snapshot labeled <u>Click Here to Learn How to Use the Snapshot Report</u>.

Other financial sites offer similar in-depth financial materials. Look for <u>Help</u> or <u>Glossary</u> when visiting other sites.

Performance over time: Quarterly and annual comparisons

Stock investors look to a company's past for clues to its future, and nothing is more crucial to this task than the comparative data from quarterly and annual reports. Looking at the year-over-year numbers tells you whether a company has been growing, and how fast.

Hoover's Online offers a free basic financial snapshot that tells you how a company's recent performance compares to that of other recent periods. To check out a quarterly performance table:

1. Go to www.hoovers.com.

2. Using the Search boxes near the top of the page, choose Search by Ticker, and type the stock symbol. (You can also choose to Search by Company if you don't know the symbol).

3. Click <u>Go</u>.

   You see a Hoover's Company Capsule on your chosen stock. This is a quick overview of a company's basics as well as the starting point for further research.

4. Click <u>Financials</u> just below the headlined company name to get quarterly and annual results.

   The next page shows a financial chart, with a list of links above it titled Free Financial Information. If the current page isn't showing quarterlies, click the <u>Quarterly Financials</u> link to call up this information.

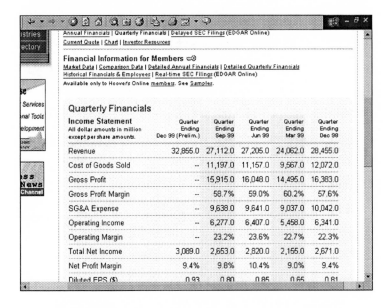

5. By examining the Income Statement, you can see whether the profit margins of the company have held steady, grown, or declined over the past year.

Below the Income Statement is a balance sheet with quarterly figures for assets and liabilities. Use the Data Definitions link at the bottom of this page to help you understand any confusing terms.

6. Click Annual Financials (at the top of the screen) to call up data in all information categories from the past three years.

Performance versus peer groups: Industry comparisons

A company's line of business can make a big difference in how investors price its shares. Sales growth and gross margins that would be stunning in discount retailing may be considered so-so or worse in software. Industry comparisons tell you how well a particular firm is doing against other company's in its peer group as well as in the general market.

These comparisons cover two types of data — stock performance and company financials. You can get a summary of both types at Market Guide (`www.marketguide.com`):

1. From the Market Guide home page, enter a stock symbol in the box at the upper left of the screen, and click Go.

This brings you to a Snapshot Report.

2. Click the Comparison link in the left-hand menu.

The tables compare each data point for the company to those of its industry as well as the *Standard & Poor's 500*, a measure of the general stock market.

Yahoo! Finance also offers company-to-industry comparison. After calling up a company snapshot:

1. Click the By link in the Research category.

2. Follow the links on this list to groups and subgroups.

For example, follow the Internet link to Internet Software, which takes to you a table of companies ranked by average analyst ratings.

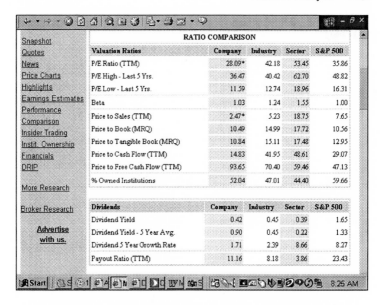

RATIO COMPARISON				
Valuation Ratios	**Company**	**Industry**	**Sector**	**S&P 500**
P/E Ratio (TTM)	28.09*	42.18	53.45	35.86
P/E High - Last 5 Yrs.	36.47	40.42	62.70	48.82
P/E Low - Last 5 Yrs.	11.59	12.74	18.96	16.31
Beta	1.03	1.24	1.55	1.00
Price to Sales (TTM)	2.47*	5.23	18.75	7.65
Price to Book (MRQ)	10.49	14.99	17.72	10.56
Price to Tangible Book (MRQ)	10.84	15.11	17.48	12.95
Price to Cash Flow (TTM)	14.83	41.95	48.61	29.07
Price to Free Cash Flow (TTM)	93.65	70.40	59.46	47.13
% Owned Institutions	52.04	47.01	44.40	59.66

Dividends	**Company**	**Industry**	**Sector**	**S&P 500**
Dividend Yield	0.42	0.45	0.39	1.65
Dividend Yield - 5 Year Avg.	0.90	0.45	0.22	1.33
Dividend 5 Year Growth Rate	1.71	2.39	8.66	8.27
Payout Ratio (TTM)	11.16	8.18	3.86	23.43

Sidebar navigation: Snapshot, Quotes, News, Price Charts, Highlights, Earnings Estimates, Performance, Comparison, Insider Trading, Instit. Ownership, Financials, DRIP, More Research, Broker Research, **Advertise with us.**

Start   8:25 AM

The Valuation Ratios table shows how the price of stock compares to its earnings, sales, book value, and cash flow. The Dividends table shows how the company's yield (price divided by annual dividend rate) compares to its peers.

Scrolling down, you find a table comparing the company's sales and profit growth rates over several time spans, and a table on financial strength, profitability, and management effectiveness.

At the bottom of the page, you find a list of other companies in the industry group. The industry groups that make up larger sectors are also listed. Keep in mind that the boundaries of industry groups and sectors shift as new technologies and types of business emerge. Also, classifications differ from site to site.

TIP

For a short list of a company's major rivals, click the Stock Comparison link after calling up a Company Profile at Quicken.com. Hoover's also lists a handful of competitors on the Company Capsule page (see the links under Top Competitors). Subscribers to Hoover's premium service can get a longer list as part of the Company Profile.

Online News Sources

The Internet is something of an echo chamber when it comes to online investment news. Surf past a few financial sites, and you're bound to see the same stories over and over. Most of these sites don't do their own reporting; instead, they package articles from news services such as Reuters, the Associated Press, and Bloomberg. They also give you plenty of corporate press releases via two services, PR Newswire and BusinessWire.

At Yahoo!, you can see the very latest stories on a company (including audio reports from ON24):

1. Call up a quote.

2. Click <u>News</u> in the More Info box.

At MSN Investor, you can go straight to the news feed from the home page:

1. Type the ticker symbol at the upper-left corner of the page.

2. Choose News from the pull-down menu and click <u>Go</u>.

For news of the market in general at MSN, see the links under Markets in the left-hand home page menu. At Yahoo! Finance, go to the links listed on the home page under Financial News (you can pick your favorite wire or press-release service here).

For free sites that do substantial reporting of their own and present the news on a readable front page, you can go to some familiar broadcasting names:

✔ CNNfn (`www.cnnfn.com`)

✔ CNBC (`www.cnbc.com`)

✔ CBS MarketWatch (`cbs.marketwatch.com`)

✔ Bloomberg's (`www.bloomberg.com`)

TheStreet.com (`www.thestreet.com`) has free material as well as material for paid subscribers. Check out Yahoo! for free news stories and commentaries from The Street.com.

News tickers

News tickers display a moving ribbon of stock prices and news headlines across your screen. Clicking a headline calls up the full story. Registered users of a site can customize the moving tickers to show news on particular stocks.

Check out news tickers at MSN Investor, Yahoo! Finance, and CNBC.com.

E-mail reports

Some financial sites deliver market reports daily — and sometimes even more frequently — via e-mail.

- ✔ CBS MarketWatch (cbs.marketwatch.com) offers several reports. To sign up for the free service, look for a signup box under the headline "Have Your News Delivered."

- ✔ InfoBeat (www.infobeat.com) e-mail service has a daily market report that you can customize to follow particular stocks. From the home page, click the <u>Finance</u> link under Customize.

Tech newsInvestor interest in the Internet (along with technology in general) has spawned Web sites focused just on tech news. These sites do plenty of original reporting and sometimes break significant stories before the mainstream media.

Here are a few leading sites:

- ✔ Upside Today (www.upside.com)
- ✔ ZDNet's "Inter@ctive Investor" (www.zdii.com)
- ✔ CNET News.com (news.cnet.com)
- ✔ Red Herring (www.redherring.com)

Conference calls

Sometimes the real news in an earnings release or other company report is in the way it's explained to analysts in conference calls. You can listen in on some of these via Yahoo!, and you can hear other recently recorded calls.

From the table of contents on Yahoo! Finance front page, click <u>Calls</u> (listed after Earnings in the Research category). You can then either hear past calls, hear the ones in progress, or get previews of upcoming calls.

Research at Company Web Sites

Most publicly traded companies have Web sites with a link containing data for investors. If you know a company's Web address, you can usually get to the investor-oriented site by clicking a link labeled something like <u>Investor Relations</u>.

On company-snapshot pages at some financial sites, look for a <u>Investor Relations</u> link.

The must-read portions of a corporate report are the management's discussion, financial statements, the accompanying notes and the auditor's report (which should be "unqualified" — finding no cause for concern). These are usually toward the end of the report, after the PR-oriented pages at the front. You can also find them in the 10K and 10Q corporate filings to the SEC. *See also* "SEC Filings."

Search Tools for Investors

To find background stories on a company, you can either do a Web-wide search, or you can focus on specific news sources.

To do a Web-wide search, type a company name in a general-purpose search engine (like Yahoo!, AltaVista, HotBot, or Northern Light) and see what turns up.

However, this type of searching can give you a lot of irrelevant hits. So this section tells you how to conduct more focused hunts.

Home-town news archives

You may be able to use home-town newspapers or publications of a company you're researching to get a close-up look at how a company is perceived in its community.

To search, locate a home-town news archive through Yahoo! Finance. (*See also* "Company Profiles" on calling up a profile from a stock quote.)

1. Find the company's physical home-office address on the Profile page.

2. Go to the Yahoo! home page.

3. Click the Newspapers link under News & Media.

4. Select By Region.

5. Select U.S. States.

6. Select a state and then cities or counties to hone in on a major newspaper (or regional business paper) that covers the area where the company you're researching is based. Use the same technique for companies outside the U.S. by choosing the Countries or Regions option in Step 5.

Major media archives

If you already subscribe to the Wall Street Journal, Barron's, or another Dow Jones Publication, you can pay slightly more to access a rich online news archive through the Wall Street Journal Interactive edition. You can search not only the Wall Street Journal itself, but also major business publications such as Fortune and Forbes.

The following are some major newspapers and magazines that provide background stories on publicly traded companies. You can search them for free and download stories (usually) for $3 or less (Forbes' stories are free):

Publication	Search Site URL
Forbes	www.forbes.com
BusinessWeek	www.businessweek.com/search.html
Red Herring	www.redherring.com
Fortune	www.pathfinder.com/fortune/archive
New York Times	archives.nytimes.com/archives
Los Angeles Times	www.latimes.com/archives
USA Today	usatoday.com/s/usatoday

 You can also get free information from Hoover's Online (www.hoover.com). The Company Capsules that you can call up often have links to recent news articles on the stock you're researching. These free stories come from newspapers as well as business magazines.

Investor-friendly search engines

Try lots of search engines to see which ones are best at ferreting out financial stories. Try searching by ticker symbol as well as company name. Try the following:

- ✔ The GO Network (www.go.com) searches by ticker symbol as well as company name. For a directory of companies by industry, as well as a list of other company-listing sites on the Web, go to www.go.com/WebDir/Business/Company_directory.

- ✔ Direct Hit (www.directhit.com) uses a popularity gauge to decide which results to list first.

- ✔ UpsideToday Research Center (www.eocenter.com/upside) is a good search engine choice if your focus is technology stocks.

 Most search engines, unless instructed otherwise, display results in order of relevance rather than date. So if you're looking for the most up-to-date news (as an investor normally would), see if the engine allows you to display the most recent items first and then refine the search terms to weed out irrelevant articles.

SEC Filings

All companies that issue shares of stock to the public must file financial data with the Securities and Exchange Commission (SEC). This includes annual and quarterly financial results and reports on any significant changes in ownership. Companies also file detailed disclosure documents to the SEC whenever they issue stock or debt.

Data direct from the SEC

Most of this financial information is available free on the Internet through an SEC's service called EDGAR (which stands for Electronic Data Gathering, Analysis, and Retrieval). The documents are made available in raw, unexcerpted form 24 hours after they're filed. Here's how to call them up:

1. Go to the SEC's home page (www.sec.gov).

2. Click <u>Search EDGAR Archives</u> at the top of the screen.

Want to know what the head honchos make? Follow the link at the bottom of the Search the EDGAR Database page for tips on where to find the executive compensation numbers.

3. Click <u>Quick Forms Lookup</u>.

4. In the Select the Form box, use the pull-down menu to select a form type, or choose All to call up all filings.

Use the <u>Click Here</u> link for more information on the form types.

5. In the company-name box, type the full company name — up to 20 characters — rather than stock symbols or abbreviations.

6. After choosing a date range, click Submit Choices.

Filings are listed by form type. Listings under each form are in chronological order, the earliest first. All forms are available in text format. Recent ones are also in HTML.

Be sure to read "Management's Discussion and Analysis of Results of Operations and Financial Condition." This is where the company is supposed to disclose any factors that may hurt its business.

In SEC filings, use the Find command in the Edit menu of your browser to locate key sections, such as the management's discussion, which always go by similar titles.

The following are SEC forms you most commonly use for research (for a full list, see www.sec.gov/edaux/forms.htm). Note that Form 144 is not available on EDGAR, nor are documents filed less than 24 hours before. Commercial services such as Edgar Online make these available to paid subscribers. *See also* "SEC data from EDGAR Online" and Part VII (for more on S-1s and initial public offerings).

The Form	Its Function
S-1	The basic registration for most public offerings of stock. It describes the company and its condition in detail.
S-1A	An amended S-1 — updated to reflect new financial results or other corporate developments since the first S-1 was filed.
SB-1	A registration form, less detailed than the S-1, for public offerings from certain small companies offering up to $10 million in securities.
Prospectus	A description of the company and its condition released at the time of a public offering. Prospectuses and amendments have file numbers starting with 424 (such as, 424A, 424B1, and so on).
Schedule 14A	A filing before corporate meetings that is required to inform shareholders on matters that will be coming up for a vote. A good source for data on executive compensation.
Form 144	A notice of the proposed sale of restricted securities — those not registered for public trading — by a company insider (form not available on EDGAR).
Form 8-K	A report of material events in a company that are significant to investors.
Form 10-K	The annual report that publicly traded companies file with the SEC. It includes financial results along with management's discussion of the firm's condition and outlook.
Form 10-Q	A quarterly report with unaudited statements of income and financial condition.
Schedule 13-D	A report filed by a person or group acquiring more than 5% of any class of shares in a publicly traded company.
Schedule 13-G	A shorter version of 13-D.

SEC data from EDGAR Online

SEC reports on the EDGAR system are raw copy, with no editing to extract the crucial data from the legal boilerplate. Commercial Web sites such as EDGAR Online take the government documents and do some editing for you, extracting the most useful investor information from SEC reports and presenting it at their own Web sites. Registered, non-paying users at EDGAR Online can get the same data available for free from the SEC's EDGAR site. Paid subscribers can also get SEC forms not in the EDGAR database and forms that have been on file less than 24 hours.

Go to www.edgaronline.com and follow the free registration procedure. Then, perform a quick search as follows:

1. From the home page, type a company symbol or name after the Quick Search By command.

2. Click Search.

The list of filings appears in reverse chronological order, with brief descriptions of the filing type.

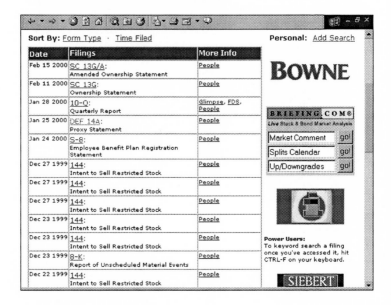

3. Click a form title.

You see a screen asking to choose the delivery format (HTML, Rich Text, or hard copy, in this case).

4. Choose HTML to display the report in two frames.

The left-hand frame has links that take you to key points of the filing on the right.

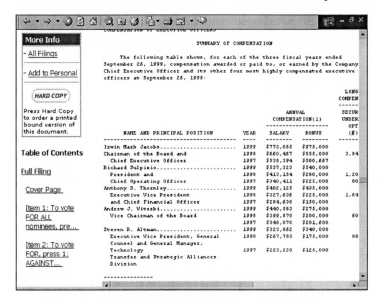

5. Use the Find function of your browser to search through the selected report and find detailed data on a particular topic.

   For example, in a proxy statement, you can get detailed data on the compensation of top executives. Use your browser's Find function to search for the word "compensation."

For companies that have recently come public, EDGAR filings in connection with the initial public offering can be a rich source of background data. *See also* Part VII.

SEC data at Yahoo!, Quicken.com, and MSN

Financial sites such as Yahoo! Finance, Quicken.com, and MSN Investor offer SEC excerpts with links to the raw filings.

At Yahoo! Finance:

1. Call up a quote.

2. Click the SEC link in the More Info box on a quote grid.

   A page shows the key parts of the most recent major SEC filing.

3. For raw SEC filings, click Raw SEC Filings on a company Profile page.

At Quicken.com:

1. Call up a quote.

2. Click the <u>SEC Filings</u> link.

At MSN Investor:

1. Call up a quote.

2. Click the <u>SEC Filings</u> link in the left-hand menu.

This calls up recent extracts. Links in the left-hand menu let you seek out key parts of the report — for example, legal issues, description of the business, or management's discussion.

3. Click All Filings to call up the raw SEC filings.

Stock Screens

A *screen* is an online program that sifts through the thousands of publicly traded stocks to find those that fit certain criteria, such as earnings growth rates, price action, or balance-sheet ratios. Depending on the type of screen, you can make your own list of criteria or use those that the screen has already selected for you.

You can find online stock screens at a variety of sites:

Site	*Stock Screen At*
AOL	Personal Finance⇨Investment Research⇨Stock Screening
Hoover's	www.hoovers.com/search/forms/stockscreener
Motley Fool	www.fool.com/stockscreens/stockscreens.htm
NASDAQ	screening.nasdaq-amex.com/screening/ NASDAQSearch.asp
Market Guide	www.marketguide.com/mgi/NETSCREEN/ Netscreen.html
Netscape	personalwealth.netscape.com/Investing/ stocks/StockScreens.html
Stockpoint	www.stockpoint.com/leftnav/pages/ stockfinder.asp
Stockpoint (advanced)	www.stockpoint.com/leftnav/pages/ stockfinderpro.asp
Yahoo!	screen.yahoo.com/stocks.html

Running ready-made screens at Quicken.com

Quicken.com offers you two different ready-made screens, for either growth or value. To run these screens at Quicken.com, follow these steps:

1. Go to the Quicken.com home page at www.quicken.com.

2. Click Investing.

3. Click Screen Stocks from the menu on the left.

4. Choose Popular Searches.

   A list of six search categories appears; each of the categories provides different growth rate and stock price ratio information.

   The categories listed under Valuation call up lists of stocks with low prices relative to their asset value, sales, and earnings, or dividends:

   - **Small Cap Value:** For smaller companies with a good three-year history.

   - **Large Cap Value:** For larger companies.

   - **High Yield:** For stocks with the highest dividends.

   The Growth categories focus on companies with better-than-average earnings for the stock price and/or superior growth rates. These include:

   - **Small Cap Growth**

   - **Large Cap Stocks**

   - **Growth Momentum**

5. Click the appropriate category.

   Each table displays the same information about each stock that is listed down the left side of the screen, including Market Cap, price-earnings (P/E) ratio, other price ratios, and growth rates.

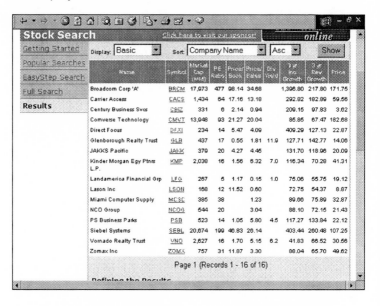

6. For more company data and news, click the trading symbol.

7. To see other data, use the Display pull-down menu at the upper left to pick another category and then click Show. The categories (and their data) that you can choose from are:

- **Company.** Price and *market cap* for each company in your screen, along with a its membership (if any) in one of the Standard & Poor's indices.

- **Growth.** The annual rate of growth in sales and earnings over the past one, three, and five years.

- **Return.** Five-year total return to stockholders, return on assets, and return on equity.

- **Valuation.** Earnings per share (EPS), market cap, P/E ratio, price/book and price/sales ratios, and dividend yield.

- **Financials.** Revenue and income per employee, current ratio and quick ratio, net profit margin, annual revenue, and long-term debt compared to equity and assets.

- **Share Info.** Current stock price, comparisons of current price to 52-week highs and lows, beta, and the percent of shares held by institutions.

Use the Sort menus to refine and organize your Quicken.com stock search. For example, if you want to see which stocks on the Large Cap Value list have the best growth characteristics, choose a growth characteristic like 5-Year Revenue or EPS Growth from the Sort menu and ask to see the list in descending order. Then click Show.

Running custom screens at MSN Investor

MSN Investor gives you the option of creating either custom screens. To create a custom screen, go to the MSN Investor home page (moneycentral.msn.com/investor/home.asp) and do the following:

1. Click <u>Finder</u> on the horizontal menu bar.

2. Click <u>Custom Search</u> in the left-hand menu. (The Pre-Defined Search link takes you to ready-made searches for stocks and mutual funds.)

If this is your first time using the Custom Search function, you may be asked to download some software. Follow the on-screen instructions to do this.

When you call up <u>Custom Search</u> and all software has been installed, you see a table with several blanks to fill in. Follow these steps to set up and run a custom screen:

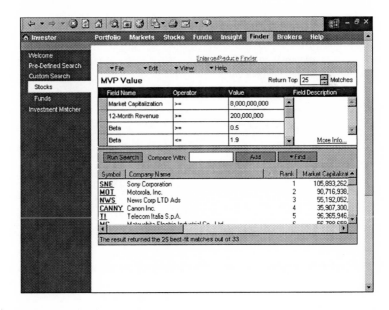

1. Click the box under Field Name to call up the search criteria menus.

   The first pull-down list shows categories such as Company Basics, Investment Return, Price Ratios, and so on.

2. Click any of these categories to see a pull-down list of specific screen criteria.

   Under Price Ratios, for instance, you find a menu with more than a dozen ratios. See the Field Description cell for a brief explanation of any field you highlight. Choose one field (or one from another pull-down list) by clicking it.

   The screen criterion you choose shows up under Field Name.

3. In the Operator column, click Choose an Operator to pick a value or range, such as =, >=, High as Possible, and so on.

   Choose Display Only if you want only the value to be shown and not used for screening.

4. In the Value column, you see Click Here to Add a Value in Red. If you have a number in mind, click the box and select Ask Me from the pull-down menu. Type a value in the highlighted space.

   To add more screen criteria, simply repeat Steps 1 to 4 to add more lines and then click Run Search.

Screening with MSN's Advisor FYI

Advisor FYI is an MSN feature alerting you to events that could significantly change the outlook for a stock. You can use it as part of your custom screen.

You can find Advisor FYI in the pull-down menu in the Field Name column. Browse through its categories and criteria to get a feel for the events you can use for screening.

For example, you can screen for stocks that have exceeded analysts' earnings estimates for the past two quarters (such upside surprises frequently point to future increases in the stock price):

1. In the left-hand column, use the pull-down menus to select the criteria you want to screen.

   For this example, choose Advisor FYI⇨Analyst Projections⇨ Exceeded Analyst Estimates for 2 Quarters.

2. Choose the specific criteria for your screen

For this example, in the Operator column, choose either Since or Not Since. By choosing Since and then selecting <In The Last Year> from the pull-down menu in the Value column, you limit your screen to stocks that have had at least two upside surprises in the past year.

Tracking Financial Analysts

To find out what analysts from investment houses and research firms are saying about a stock, you can choose either broad summaries (usually free) or detailed reports (for a fee).

Free reports

Zacks and First Call are two major names you encounter when looking for analyst reports. You can find free analyst survey data at several financial sites.

At Yahoo! Finance, you can get a Zacks report on analysts' ratings and earnings estimates by clicking Research on the Profile page or in the More Info box of a quote.

Zacks gives you both the latest average ranking (on a one-to-five scale) and earnings estimates, updated weekly, along with previous numbers. A Zacks report allows you to spot an upward or downward trend that may influence the company's stock price.

For example, you can use the earnings projections in a Zacks report to calculate a stock's forward P/E — its current price divided by expected earnings.

✔ The P/E in quotes, also called trailing P/E, is based on the past four-quarters' earnings.

✔ For fast-growing companies, the forward P/E can be much lower (and can sound more realistic) than the trailing P/E. Bear in mind, though, that it's based only on forecasts, not money in the bank.

You can also find a few free analyst reports at Multex Investor (**see also** "Full reports and briefs" for more Multex features). Multex Investor offers average earnings estimates and rankings from Media General Financial services. Go to `www.multexinvestor.com` and type a stock symbol in the Search box on the home page. The earnings and ranking data appears with a list of recent analyst reports. First-time users need to register for this free service.

As you read various analysts' reports you encounter terms like buy, hold, and outperform. Different firms mean different things by these terms. To help understand what analysts are saying, check out the Yahoo! list of equity rating systems at biz.yahoo.com/f/bc.html#ratings.

Upgrades and downgrades

You can see how a stock has been faring among analysts at brokerages and research firms by going to a list of upgrades and downgrades. These lists are changes in the rating on a stock — when an analyst decides it's time to tell clients to buy, hold, or (rarely) sell.

At Yahoo!, click Upgrade/Downgrade History on a stock's Profile page.

You can also get the most recent upgrades, downgrades, and initial coverage for the whole universe of stocks by using the following sites:

✔ At the Yahoo! Finance home page, click the Up/Downgrades link in the Research list.

✔ At MSN Investor, click Up/Downgrades under Markets in the left-hand menu of the homepage.

✔ Look for similarly-named links at other sites.

Full reports and briefs

If you want to know *why* analysts rank stocks as they do, you can find thousands of full-text reports at the Multex Investor site. To see a list of full reports available for a particular stock:

1. Go to the Multex Investor site at www.multexinvestor.com.

2. Type the ticker symbol in the search box on the Multex home page.

You see a list of free and pay-per-view reports:

• **Free reports,** listed first, are either from Multex directly or from brokerage firms offering them as promotions. When you view a free report from a brokerage firm, expect to fill out a form so that a broker can locate you to drum up some business.

• **Pay-per-view reports** are generally the work of brokers and independent research firms. Some are in the sub-$10 range, but others are priced only for very serious investors.

Part IV

Shopping for a Broker

Online investors have plenty of choice in brokers, from full-service to barebones and everything in between. Figuring out which ones offer the services you need at the best prices can be tricky, though. This part covers brokers from soup to nuts.

In this part . . .

Broker Ratings

There's more to broker costs than commissions, and there's more to service than stock trades.

Depending on the type of investor you are, you may need more than the basics, or you may be content with low rates and a broker that leaves you to do your own planning and research.

Online broker rating sites can help you pick out the firms with a package that strikes the right balance between cost and service. These sites can also give you some idea of how well all of the brokers carry out essential functions, such as executing trades and answering the phone quickly when you need help.

The following sites differ somewhat in methods, rankings, and the number of brokers covered:

✔ **SmartMoney.com:** Go to www.smartmoney.com/si/brokers to see rates for both discount and a few full-service brokers. This site focuses on a relatively few large firms (21 discounters and 8 full-service firms in one recent update), but has tools to help you pick firms that fit your needs and investing style. See the Which Broker Is Best for You? links.

✔ **Gomez Advisors:** Go to www.gomezadvisors.com and then click Brokers. Gomez covers a wide range of brokers (more than 50 in one recent update) and ranks them by performance measures, such as ease of use and customer confidence, and also by investor type.

✔ **OnLine Investment Services:** Go to www.sonic.net/donaldj to see the largest number of brokers (more than 80 at recent count) and new reports every month or so.

Click Choosing a Discount Broker for an especially useful report that breaks down the field into several categories, such as brokers for experienced investors, brokers for novices, brokers with lots of fee-free mutual funds, and so on.

✔ **Kiplinger.com:** Go to www.kiplinger.com/investments and click Broker Rankings. The list of brokers is not large (approximately 30), but the page enables you to easily rank them by several important categories, such as commissions and broker knowledge.

To get the most out of the ratings offered by the preceding sites, you need to know what to look for and what to expect. Visit the Motley Fool's Discount Broker Center (www.fool.com) for a good overview of the broker search process. From the site's home page, choose Discount Brokers from the Quick Find menu (scroll to the

Pers. Finance section) on the right-hand side of the screen. You find a series of articles on topics such as choosing a broker, using your account, and account security.

Choosing between Full-Service and Discount Brokers

Until recently, you could draw a clear line in the brokerage business:

- ✔ **Full-service houses** featured commissioned broker-salespeople, full plates of financial products, and high rates.

- ✔ **Discounters** featured low rates, a focus mainly on stock trading, and no sales pressure.

After Internet trading hit the scene, the rush to sign up customers blurred that line almost beyond recognition.

To see how full-service and discount brokers compare these days, go to SmartMoney magazine's rating site, which divides brokers into two groups, discount/online and full-service, and ranks the major firms in both. *See also* "Broker Ratings" in this part for more information.

 Another way to go about choosing a broker is to decide what kind of investor you really are, based on your personality, plans, and experience and then select a firm that fits your personality. *See also* Part I.

Evaluating Online Broker Service

How much you demand from an online site depends in part on your confidence as an investor and your fondness for darting around on the Web.

- ✔ Some brokerages stress one-stop shopping, with stocks, bonds, funds, options, retirement plans, financial planning tools, research, quotes, charts, and portfolio tracking all at one site.

- ✔ Others stress fast, cheap stock trading and assume you can get your data guidance elsewhere.

 One way to get the best of both worlds — dirt-cheap trading and a full basket of services — is to have two online accounts, one at a deep-discounter and another at an online firm with higher commissions and more features.

The following are some of the key measures of quality service at online brokerage sites.

Customer support

Rating services and bulletin boards have plenty to say about customer service (*see also* "Message and Bulletin Boards" in this part). The fast growth of many online brokers has strained their capacity to handle trades on the Internet, so customers sometimes have to resort to the phone to make trades, get account data, or correct errors.

You can rank brokers specifically by customer support at Gomez Advisors and Kiplinger.com:

✔ **Gomez Advisors**

> *1.* Go to www.gomezadvisors.com.
>
> *2.* Click Brokers and then click Customer Confidence under the heading "Who Is the Best Online Broker?"

✔ **Kiplinger.com**

> *1.* Go to www.kiplinger.com.
>
> *2.* Click Broker Rankings and choose Responsiveness under the Or Sort By menu.
>
> *3.* Click Sort the List.

IPOs

Online investors (and small investors in general) used to have little chance of getting in on high-quality initial public offerings. That situation is changing fast, and you can participate in at least some IPOs at many online sites.

You can screen Kiplinger.com's list of online brokers to exclude those that don't yet offer IPOs:

1. Go to www.kiplinger.com.

2. Click Broker Rankings and choose any sorting option from the Or Sort By menu.

3. Check the box marked IPOs to exclude those that don't yet offer IPOs.

4. Click Sort the List.

This simple screen doesn't tell you how many IPOs a broker offers and what restrictions they place on participation. Check out the broker's Web site for more details. *See also* Part VII.

Mutual funds

Don Johnson's Choosing a Discount Broker page tells which online brokers offer commission-free mutual fund trading. Many firms offer additional mutual funds for a fee, usually about the size of their stock commission or slightly higher. *See also* "Choosing Between Discount and Full-Service Brokers" and Part VIII.

If you want to do most or all of your investing at one site, pick a brokerage that offers a wide range of choices in mutual funds. Check the visitor's portion of the broker's Web site to see the list of funds offered.

And if you have your eye on a particular fund that you want to buy, try looking it up at MSN Investor, which tracks the availability of funds at online brokers. Follow these steps:

1. Go to moneycentral.msn.com/investor.

2. Click Funds on the horizontal menu bar.

3. Type the trading symbol of a fund (or use the Find program to look it up).

4. Click Go.

A fund quote rating summary appears.

5. Click Fund Facts in the left-hand menu.

An Investment Overview page, which includes a Broker Availability list, appears.

 The SmartMoney site ranks brokers in both full-service and discount categories by their mutual-fund offerings:

1. Go to www.smartmoney.com/si/brokers.

2. Choose Our Latest Rankings under either the discount or full-service category.

Each service category has a link to mutual fund rankings.

Planning and tracking tools

You may need some help developing an investment strategy and then tracking your stocks, bonds, and funds to see if you're on your way to meeting your goals. You also may need some help at tax time calculating your capital gains and losses.

To look for online brokerages that have the tools for these tasks, you can start with the ranking for onsite resources at Gomez Advisors:

1. Go to www.gomezadvisors.com.

2. Click Brokers in the left-hand menu.

3. Click <u>On-Site Resources</u> under the heading, Who Is the Best Online Broker?

4. Click the <u>Review</u> link and read any reviews that interest you.

5. Visit any broker's site to check out the programs.

Free real-time quotes

If you want to find just the right time to buy and sell, you may want a broker with unrestricted free quotes in real time. Many brokers limit the number of free real-time quotes to a certain number (100 or 50, for example) per trade. Similar restrictions may be placed on automated phone quotes.

Don Johnson has a section on brokers offering free real-time quotes, unrestricted and otherwise, in his lists at his page, Choosing a Discount Broker (www.sonic.net/donaldj). Click <u>Help in Choosing a Discount Stock Broker.</u>

Alerts and updates

How well does an online broker get important information to you when you need it?

✔ Gomez ranks brokers on the quality of their news alerts and real-time updates of account holdings. Under the Who Is the Best Online Broker? heading, click <u>Relationship Services</u> and read the reviews for details.

✔ Kiplinger.com ranks brokers by the clarity of their account statements.

1. Go to kiplinger.com/investments.

2. Click Broker Rankings.

3. Choose Statement Clarity in the Or Sort By menu.

4. Click Sort the List.

See also Part VI.

Bonds and other alternatives to stocks

Along with plenty of mutual funds to choose from, you should have access to bonds and options to diversify your portfolios and defend against stock-market downturns.

✔ E*TRADE (www.etrade.com) has a site for trading corporate bonds, Treasuries, municipal bonds, and other government bonds (including zero-coupon bonds).

✔ With the Kiplinger.com broker rating screen
(www.kiplinger.com), you can screen out brokers that don't
offer bonds. Just check the boxes marked Corporate Bonds,
Municipal Bonds, and Treasuries.

See also Part IX for more about various types of bonds.

Options are appropriate only for sophisticated traders, but even a
relative beginner with an eye on the future might want to look for
option-trading potential in an online broker.

✔ On the Kiplinger.com rating screen (www.kiplinger.com),
check the Options box and narrow the list to brokers that offer
online option trading.

✔ Don Johnson's Choosing a Discount Broker (www.sonic.net/
donaldj) offers detailed data on brokers' costs and range of
offerings. Be sure to scroll to the Best Brokers for Options
section.

Online speed and reliability

An online site should be easy to use and reliable. You shouldn't
spend a lot of time waiting for screens to load, trades to clear, and
data to be refreshed.

You can find out about the speed and reliability of brokers by visiting message boards, like those run by The Motley Fool. *See also*
"The Motley Fool's Discount Broker message board" in the part.

For a more scientific gauge of a site's speed and reliability, use the
following tools for tracking broker performance:

✔ At the Gomez broker rating page (www.Gomez.com):

1. Choose a broker from the How Are the Brokers Performing
pull-down menu.

2. Click Submit.

You see figures for response times on the broker's home
page and in its secure sites (those reached after you log in).
Each figure is compared to an average.

3. Click eCommerce Performance Monitor for more detailed
data, including speedometer-type gauges.

✔ At SmartMoney, use the Web Reliability category to rank discount and online brokers:

1. Go to www.smartmoney.com/si/brokers/discount.

2. Click Web Reliability, or click the link <u>Broker Meter: How Fast
Is Your Broker?</u>

A graphic comparison of online brokers in several areas, such as page download and connection setup time, appears.

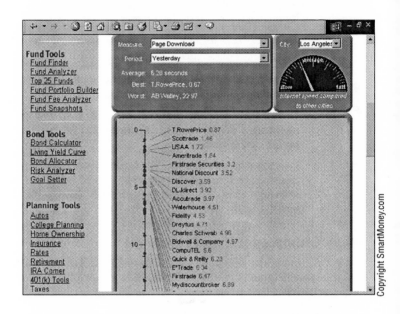

3. Use the Measure pull-down menu to choose the specific area you want to compare; use the Period pull-down menu to choose when the measurement was taken; or use the City pull-down menu to choose one of seven major cities where measurements were made.

Brokerages are instantly re-ranked when you change any of these criteria. *Note:* You can also compare cities to see which has the slower and faster Internet speeds.

Message and Bulletin Boards

Message and bulletin boards can be a useful source of insight into online behavior if you keep a few caveats in mind:

✔ Nobody's perfect, and the more customers a broker has, the more likely it is that a customer will have a problem and advertise it on the Internet.

✔ Message boards don't usually give you both sides of the story.

✔ You don't know the source of a message — it could be posted by a company shill or disgruntled ex-employee.

✔ Many complaints you read may come from people (such as day-traders) who demand types of service that just aren't relevant to you.

You may also want to keep track of the problem brokers report at Don Johnson's OnLine Investment Services (`www.sonic.net/donaldj`).

The really serious complaints about brokers go to regulators, litigation, or arbitration. *See also* "Spotting Broker Trouble" in this part for tips on tracking down these cases.

The Motley Fool's Discount Broker message board

Use the Motley Fool's message boards to get the lowdown on discount brokers:

1. Go to `www.fool.com`.

2. Click Discount Brokers on the Quick Find pull-down menu.

3. Click Discount Broker Message Board.

4. Use the Search box at the top of the page to look for information about specific brokers.

You can also post your own messages after registering (for free) at the Fool's home page. See the Registration link in the Access the Fool area.

Consumer ratings at Gomez Advisors

Utilize Gomez Advisors message board by doing the following:

1. Go to `www.gomezadvisors.com`.

2. Click Brokers.

3. Go to the box labeled Consumer Ratings & Reviews.

4. Choose a broker and click Go, or (for an unsorted list of new mail), choose Click to see most recent posts.

When you call up a message, Gomez gives you a link to customer ratings of the brokerage firm. You can also fill out a rating form of your own.

Spotting Broker Trouble

No one can guarantee that you won't lose money in the stock market, but you have a right to fair dealings from brokers and the firms that employ them.

Remember: All investors can complain to regulators and seek damages (usually through arbitration). The complaints of other investors are put on the record, and they may tip you off to potential problems when you're shopping for a broker.

This section covers the main sources of background data on brokers and brokerage firms.

Broker backgrounds at NASD Regulation

NASD Regulation Inc. is an independent arm of the National Association of Securities Dealers (NASD) that regulates the securities industry and the NASDAQ Stock Market.

After you narrow your search for potential brokerages down to a few names, run a background check by using NASD's online search program that retrieves enforcement files on brokers and firms. Follow these steps:

 1. Go to the NASD Regulation home page at www.nasdr.com.

 2. Click About Your Broker, or choose About Your Broker from the pull-down menu and click Go!

     A page that explains NASD Regulations Public Disclosure Program and contains links to searches and more information appears. The What Is Disclosable? link, for example, explains what kind of events are on file for brokers and firms.

 3. Click Perform an On-Line Search.

     A legal disclaimer form appears.

 4. Click Agree.

     A page appears that asks you whether you're an ordinary investor or acting in some other capacity, such as media or law enforcement.

 5. Click the appropriate label — Broker or Firm — from the pull-down menu.

     If you're shopping for online investing sites rather than checking out a particular financial advisor or broker, choose Firm.

 6. If you're searching for a firm, type its name in the box to the right of Firm Name and pick Begins With from the menu to get the best chance of a match.

 7. Click Begin .Search for Firm.

     A list of firm names appears as a result of your search.

 8. Click the firm that you're looking for.

Note that one parent company (such as Fidelity) can have several different subsidiaries, such as mutual-fund management — in addition to its brokerage. Be sure to click the brokerage unit.

A page appears that includes links to data on the firm's location, legal status (corporation, partnership, and so on), business lines, and registrations (such as states in which it can legally operate).

If the <u>Maybe</u> link appears after Disclosure Events, NASD Regulation may have enforcement actions or complaints in the firm's file.

9. Click Deliver Report on the menu bar at the top of the page to get an e-mail-based report on the firm.

10. After filling out a brief form, you can click buttons at the bottom of the page to start a new search for a broker or firm, clear your delivery form, or end the session.

SEC investor resources

The U.S. Securities and Exchange Commission's Web site (www.sec.gov) has several useful links to investors who want to check out a brokerage, broker, or financial advisor.

1. From the home page, click Investor Assistance & Complaints.

2. Click Protect Your Money.

A page with several links to consumer information appears.

- The <u>Complaints</u> link takes you to a site that tells you what to do in case you feel your broker or firm has cheated you or broken the law.

- The <u>Check Out</u> link tells your where to go for background checks on brokers, advisors, and their firms (including NASD Regulation and state securities regulators).

- The <u>Avoid Trouble</u> link takes you to a series of articles on the risk of online trading, the mechanics of trade executions, and the warning signs of investment cyberscams.

- The <u>SEC Enforcement Actions</u> link tells you what the SEC has been doing and whether your broker or firm has been in trouble.

On the page that appears after you click the SEC Enforcement Actions link, these links are of particular interest:

- <u>Litigation Releases</u> offers a chronological list of SEC civil and criminal cases in federal court against brokers, advisors, and firms.

- <u>Administrative Proceedings</u> offers a list of administrative actions started or settled by the SEC.

- <u>Search SEC Information</u> enables you to search the SEC database for a particular firm or individual. Type the name in the search box and press Enter. The list of hits can include files not related to civil or criminal SEC action.

Choose Edit⇨Find from your browser menu to search for a particular firm or individual in SEC files that you encounter as you do your research.

Getting help from state regulators

Along with federal SEC watchdogs, state governments also enforce securities laws covering firms and brokers operating within their borders. Laws, consumer disclosure, and online access vary from state to state, as does the label of the state agency charged with securities regulation.

To locate your state's regulator:

1. Go to the Web site of the North American Securities Administrators Association at `www.nasaa.org`.

2. Click Find Your Securities Regulator.

3. Click the country you want to search. If you're looking for a state in the U.S., click <u>United States</u>.

4. Choose a state from the Show Office pull-down menu. This page also has a U.S. map. Go directly to the agency addresses and other data by clicking a state.

5. Click Show Office.

The addresses, phone numbers, and Web addresses (if available) of the state regulatory offices are displayed, along with names of top officials.

Arbitration records

As part of its broker rating system, SmartMoney magazine ranks firms by their record of disputes that go to arbitration. The more a brokerage has to pay out to disgruntled investors, the lower the score. (SmartMoney makes allowances for the size of the firm and the number of accounts.)

To see the ratings:

1. Go to `www.smartmoney.com/si/brokers`.

2. Click <u>Our Latest Rankings</u> for either discount or full-service brokers.

3. Click <u>Staying Out of Trouble</u>. You see SmartMoney's listing of the best and worst brokers based on the number of arbitration awards as well as state and federal regulatory actions.

Watching Costs

The most obvious cost for an investor in the stock market is the commission, the amount charged by a broker on each sale and purchase of stocks, bonds and, in some cases, mutual funds. It's the figure that gets the most publicity (at least in discount brokerage ads), and it's clearly important for active traders.

You can find a regularly updated list of trading commissions for discount brokers at Don Johnson's OnLine Investment Services (www.sonic.net/donaldj). Check out the link <u>See the Latest Discount Stock Brokers Ranked Report</u>. ***See also*** "Broker Ratings," in this part.

In some cases, brokers charge different commissions for market and limit orders. Johnson has separate rankings for both types:

✔ See www.sonic.net/donaldj/limit.html for limit-order ranking.

✔ See www.sonic.net/donaldj/market.html for the ranks based on market orders.

Commissions aren't the whole story, especially if you're taking advantage of services (such as IRAs or margin trading) beyond simple stock trading in a cash account. This section lists other costs to watch.

Margin loan rates

If you borrow against stock or other assets on your account to buy shares, the broker charges interest on the amount not covered by your cash balance.

✔ **Don Johnson's** Choosing a Discount Broker page, at www.sonic.net/donaldj/query.html, sorts the rates into four categories from Best (Lowest) to Too High for Small Accounts.

✔ **Kiplinger.com** shows margin rates for a smaller number of online brokers. To check out the Kiplinger.com ratings:

1. Go to www.kiplinger.com/investments.

2. Click the <u>Broker Rankings</u> link.

   This takes you to a screen where you can pull up data, including margin interest, on brokers.

✔ **Gomez Advisors** combines commissions and margin rates to come up with a ranking of lowest-cost brokers.

1. Go to `www.gomezadvisors.com`.

2. Click the Brokers channel.

3. Click <u>Overall Cost</u> under the heading, Who Is the Best Online Broker?

Mutual fund fees

You can buy and sell mutual funds through many brokers rather than going directly to the fund itself. However, brokers vary in the range of funds they offer and in how many they let you trade for no additional fee. *See also* "Evaluating Online Broker Service" in this part.

The Mutual Funds section of Don Johnson's (`www.sonic.net/donaldj`) Choosing a Discount Broker page gives a quick overview of these mutual-fund policies.

Miscellaneous fees

Some brokers charge annual fees or set-up fees for retirement accounts (such as IRAs) and special services (such as registering shares in an owner's name — a requirement for dividend reinvestment plans).

✔ The SmartMoney site includes miscellaneous fees in its rating of overall costs for full-service brokers. Go to `smartmoney.com/si/brokers/fullserv` and then click Commissions and Fees.

✔ Don Johnson (`www.sonic.net/donaldj`) covers IRA fees in his Choosing a Discount Broker page.

Assisted trades

When you set up an online account, you may think you'll never talk to a live person again. But don't be so sure. Internet trading systems sometimes break down under the weight of heavy volume. Your online broker should have automated phone trading or live order-takers available at such times. These assisted trades usually cost more than online trades. Don Johnson's (`www.sonic.net/donaldj`) Choosing a Discount Broker page notes assisted-trade rates in his broker descriptions.

Check with brokers themselves to get the most up-to-date cost information before deciding to open an account.

Part V

Trading Online

Although online trading sites differ in look and feel from brokerage to brokerage, the essentials of buying and selling stock are the same at all of them. The following part describes how to set up accounts, trade stocks, and keep records online. You also see how you can go online to locate stock purchase opportunities that don't involve going through a broker.

In this part . . .

Buying and Selling Shares

Generally, buying or selling stocks online is a four-step process:

1. Determine how much money you have in your account to make the trade.

2. Complete an online trading form.

3. Review the order.

4. Send your order to your broker for execution.

Along the way, you have several choices to make — whether to buy, sell, or sell short, whether to trade at the current market price or set a different one, and whether to place special conditions on the order's timing and execution.

The speed of online stock trading presents special risks, such as impulsive buying and selling. All investors should read the Securities and Exchange Commission's brief guide to online investing at `www.sec.gov/consumer/onlitips.html` for more information.

This section covers the trading of stock that *isn't* involved in an initial public offering. For buying IPOs, see Part VII. For buying and selling mutual funds and index securities online, see Part VIII. For trading bonds, see Part IX.

Account balance and buying power

Before you buy stock, online or off, you need to make sure you have enough money in your account to pay for your purchase at settlement time — the third business day after the transaction.

To verify that you have enough money in a new cash account:

1. Log on to your brokerage site and click a link labeled Account Balances, Account Summary, or something similar.

2. Before making a purchase, check that your broker has received the money you sent and has put it in the cash vehicle you chose, such as a money market fund.

When working with a cash account, remember the following:

✔ After you buy securities (or transfer them into the account), you see two numbers in your basic account balance statement. One is the total value of all securities; the other is cash available for buying.

- ✔ If the cost of the stock you want to buy is more than your cash balance, you can sell other securities at the same time you make the purchase. In that case, go to a link, usually labeled <u>Positions</u>, that lists separate securities and how much you own of each (100 shares of XYZ, 50 shares of ABC, and so on). This list tells you how much of which stocks, bonds, or mutual funds you have to sell to raise the needed cash.

When working with a margin account, remember the following:

- ✔ Your available maximum is called your buying power. This is a figure based on margin requirements (set by regulators, stock markets, and brokers) and your account equity — the total cash and market value minus any borrowed amounts.

- ✔ For stocks bought on margin, the account equity after the purchase must be at least 50 percent of the shares' market value. So, for example, if your account consisted of $5,000 in cash, your buying power would be $10,000. That is, you could borrow another $5,000 on margin to buy shares worth $10,000, leaving your equity (market value minus the loan) at $5,000.

Market orders

The simplest type of order is a market order, in which you instruct your broker to buy or sell a stock as soon as possible at the best available price.

Market orders require the fewest steps but carry a significant risk. In a volatile market (or if your particular stock is just having a volatile day), the actual price you pay can be different from the price at the time you place the order.

To get a feel for market orders and other types of trading without using real money or opening an account, take the test drive at the Morgan Stanley Dean Witter Online site, which has an order process similar to other online brokers (check your online broker's <u>Help</u> or <u>Education</u> links for further information). Go to the home page at www.online.msdw.com and follow these steps.

1. Under the heading Test Drive Our Demo, click the <u>See for Your-self</u> link.

A page labeled Demo - Investor Center appears. The page features a horizontal menu of links.

2. Click Trading.

A stock-trading page called Demo — Stock Order appears.

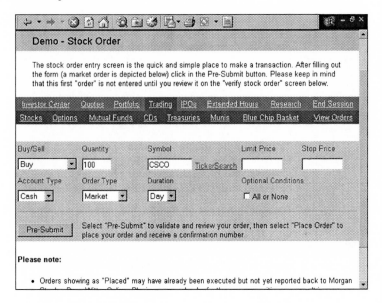

The stock order entry screen is the quick and simple place to make a transaction. After filling out the form (a market order is depicted below) click in the Pre-Submit button. Please keep in mind that this first "order" is not entered until you review it on the "verify stock order" screen below.

| Investor Center | Quotes | Portfolio | Trading | IPOs | Extended Hours | Research | End Session |

| Stocks | Options | Mutual Funds | CDs | Treasuries | Munis | Blue Chip Basket | View Orders |

| Buy/Sell | Quantity | Symbol | | Limit Price | Stop Price |
| Buy | 100 | CSCO | TickerSearch | | |

| Account Type | Order Type | Duration | Optional Conditions |
| Cash | Market | Day | ☐ All or None |

Pre-Submit — Select "Pre-Submit" to validate and review your order, then select "Place Order" to place your order and receive a confirmation number.

Please note:

- Orders showing as "Placed" may have already been executed but not yet reported back to Morgan

---

3. From the Buy/Sell pull-down menu, choose the transaction type: either Buy or Sell.

   See also "Short sales" in this part for more on the Sell Short and Buy to Cover choices in this menu.

4. From the Account Type pull-down menu, choose Cash or Margin (if you're borrowing to buy shares and your account permits this).

   Regardless of whether you're using a cash or margin account, you place an order in the same way. However, with a margin account remember:

   - You can buy up only to your buying power — your total available cash plus any additional amount you're allowed to borrow.

   - The broker automatically lends you the amount you spend beyond your available cash; you then pay interest on this loan at the margin rate. *See also* Part IV for more on brokers' margin rates.

   - The risks in margin trading are that you can lose more than you spent to buy the stock, and that you may be forced to sell the stock at a loss and then raise cash to cover the loan if its value falls below the minimum maintenance level (a value set by regulators, stock exchanges, and brokers).

5. From the Quantity drop-down list, type the number of shares you want to buy or sell.

6. From the Order Type drop-down list, choose Market.

7. Type the stock ticker in the Symbol field (or click <u>Ticker Search</u> to look it up).

8. From the Duration drop-down list, select Day — your only choice for a market order.

    Selecting Day means the order must be executed no later than the end of that trading day. (Most market orders close in a few seconds.)

9. Click the Pre-Submit button.

    A Verify Stock Order page appears. This is your last chance to check the current price and change your mind on a market order. You can also see your stock order and the total estimated price — shares plus commission.

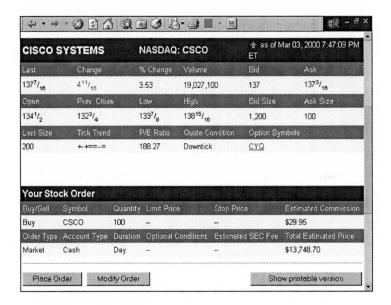

10. Click the Place Order button to go ahead with the transaction, or click Modify Order to change it.

    A screen with your order confirmation number and instructions on checking it appears.

11. Click View Open Orders to see whether your order has closed.

If you place a market order in a volatile market, you may find that the price you end up paying is a bit higher or lower than the estimated price you saw earlier. *See also* "Limit orders" and "Stop and stop-limit orders" in this part for transactions in which, unlike market orders, you can name a price.

Limit orders

A limit order puts a ceiling or floor on the price you'll accept when you buy or sell a stock.

✔ For purchases, the limit price is how high you'll go. The broker must buy at that price or lower.

✔ For sales, the limit price is the lowest you'll accept. The broker must sell at that price or higher.

Limit orders give you a measure of security because you know you can't pay more or receive less than the amount you specify.

Use limit orders to limit some of the risk in buying and selling a volatile stock. For example, if you like the longer-term outlook for a company but think its price is too high right now, you can place a limit order at a lower price to catch it on the next downswing (if there is one).

The Morgan Stanley Dean Witter Online demo for limit orders is similar to what you see at other online broker sites (check your online broker's Help or Education links for further information). Follow the steps for a market order (see the preceding section "Market orders"), but make the following changes:

1. From the Order Type drop-down list, choose Limit.

2. From the Duration drop-down list, choose GTC, which stands for Good Until Canceled. This keeps the order open for up to 60 days, and you can cancel it before then.

3. In the Limit Price text box, specify a per-share price either below the current quote (for a buy) or above it (for a sell).

4. In the Optional Conditions area, you can instruct the broker to fill the whole order in one trade by checking the All or None checkbox. With the All or None option, remember:

• The All or None option usually applies only to larger orders (usually 300 shares or more) for stocks with low trading volume.

• Checking All or None sets a further restriction on the transaction. Thus, it may increase the chances that the trade will not happen at all. On the other hand, if your broker has to make the trade in stages, you can be charged commissions on each separate trade.

You can also use limit orders for buying and selling stocks outside normal trading hours and on electronic communications networks (ECNs). *See also* "Trading after Hours" later in this part.

Stop and stop-limit orders

Like a limit order, a stop order also sets a price — but with a different function. The stop price acts as a trigger. When the stock rises or falls to that point, the broker immediately executes a market order. (As a market order, the actual transaction price may be different from the stop price.)

Stops are commonly used for two reasons:

- ✔ You can use a sell stop order (also called a stop-loss order) to get out of a stock automatically if it falls to a certain point. If you own a stock that has risen sharply, you may choose to set a stop order 10 or 15 percent below the current price to protect most of your profits in case the price starts falling.

- ✔ If you're selling short, you can place a buy stop order to cut your losses if a stock that you've sold short rises in value. *See* the section, "Short sales," in this part for more on this process.

A stop-limit order combines stop and limit prices to trigger buys and sells within a specified range. By placing a stop-limit sale order at a limit price of 15 and a stop price of 15¼, you tell your broker to execute a sale once the price drops to 15¼, but not to sell it below 15.

The Morgan Stanley Dean Witter Online demo for limit orders is similar to what you see at other online broker sites (check your online broker's <u>Help</u> or <u>Education</u> links for further information). Follow the steps for a market order (*see* the section "Market orders"), but make the following changes:

1. From the Order Type drop-down list, choose Stop.

2. Type a value in the Stop Price text box.

3. If you're placing a stop buy order to close out a short position (that is, to buy back shares that you've borrowed and sold short), choose Buy to Cover from Buy/Sell drop-down list. (If that choice isn't listed, simply choose Buy.)

For a stop-limit order, make all the preceding changes and add a limit price in the Limit Price box as well.

Unlike market orders, stop and stop-limit orders slow down the transaction process enough to allow changes and cancellations. *See also* "Canceling or Changing Orders" later in this part.

Short sales

A short sale is a way to make money from falling prices. You borrow shares from your broker and sell them, hoping to buy them back later at a lower price. Because such trades require a loan (of shares, not cash), they require you to have a margin account. *See also* "Mail-in applications" later in this part for more on margin accounts.

Look up information on short sales in your online broker's <u>Help</u> or <u>Education</u> links for details on the risks involved. The major risk is that you can lose money from rising prices — and unlike falling values, which can go no lower than zero, price hikes have no upper limit.

The Morgan Stanley Dean Witter Online demo for limit orders is similar to what you see at other online broker sites (check your online broker's <u>Help</u> or <u>Education</u> links for further information). To place a short sale, follow the steps for a market order (*see* the section "Market orders"), but make the following changes:

1. From the Buy/Sell drop-down list, choose Sell Short.

2. From the Account Type drop-down list, choose Short. (At some brokers, you may have to choose Margin if that is the only choice listed other than Cash.)

3. You can set a limit price for the short sale. But a short sale order (like a market order) cannot be extended past the trading day, so the stock does not have much time to reach your desired price.

Under stock exchange rules, a stock must be headed up in price (or be holding steady after a gain) before you can sell it short. This "up-tick rule" was put in place after the 1987 market crash to keep short sales from accelerating the downward move of a stock.

Buying back borrowed shares works like a short sale in reverse — if your strategy has worked, you're buying low after selling high. At many brokers, you simply choose "Buy" to carry out one of these trades. But at the Morgan Stanley Dean Witter site, you choose Buy to Cover from the Buy/Sell menu.

Short sellers commonly set stop prices for these trades to nail down profits. If a stock you shorted at $80 falls to $50, you might set a stop buy order at $60. Even if you have to buy at that level, you'll still close out your short position $20 ahead.

For a good overview of all types of trades covered in this section, go to E*TRADE's Learning Center, which is open to visitors as well as customers. At the home page (www.etrade.com), do the following:

1. Click Help in the upper menu.

2. Use the search window that appears to look up a term, or you can browse the Learning Center table of contents.

   Check out the <u>Making Trades</u> link for topics such as short selling, stop and limit orders, margin trading, and so on.

Canceling or Changing Orders

With limit or stop-limit orders, you can change or cancel an unfilled order by going to the order-viewing page. You can also do this with market orders placed after trading hours (these wouldn't have been executed until the next day). For market orders placed during the trading day, the chances of calling them back are slim to none.

To cancel or change an order:

1. Look for a link labeled <u>View Orders</u>, <u>View Open Orders</u>, <u>Order Status</u>, or something similar.

   Clicking these links shows you whether your order is still unfilled or whether it has been executed.

2. If the order is still open, look for a button or link that enables you to change or cancel your order, and then click the appropriate button or link.

   If your broker has an alert program, you should get a message as soon as the order is filled.

Don't assume that an order listed as "open" can be changed or cancelled. When you submit an order to a broker, the broker sends it on to the market to be filled by dealers or exchange specialists. By the time your broker gets your request to change or cancel, it may be too late for the broker to call it back. Always check to see whether an order has been canceled before making a new one. Otherwise, you risk making two buys when you meant to make one — and maybe owing your broker a lot of money.

Day Trading

True _day trading_ — the buying and selling of stocks and other securities within one market session — is an activity for full-time professionals and is beyond the scope of this book. It's also beyond the scope of most online investors, who lack the data and sophisticated software needed to make informed decisions in this rapid-fire way. Unfortunately, the speed of the Internet and its wealth of information can fool you into thinking you're faster and better informed than you really are.

For sound information on day trading, check out the following:

- ✔ The SEC's Web site
  (`www.sec.gov/consumer/search.html`): From the home page, click <u>Day Trading</u> and read:
  - The <u>Day Trading: Your Dollars at Risk</u> link for SEC caveats.
  - The <u>Problem Gambling</u> link, featuring a self-scoring test of your trading behavior.
- ✔ The Rookie Day Trader site (`www.rookiedaytrader.com`).

Remember: Some of the risks of day trading, such as the danger of developing a gambling problem or of getting carried away with euphoria or panic of the market, also lurk in ordinary online investing. If you spend much of the day at a computer checking your stocks and making frequent trades, you may fall into destructive behavior patterns even if you're not day trading in a classic sense.

Direct Stock Purchase Plans

Well over a thousand U.S. companies have some program for selling shares directly to investors rather than through stock markets and brokers.

- ✔ *Dividend Reinvestment Plans,* or DRIPs, allow current shareholders to take dividends in stock shares rather than cash and, usually, to buy extra shares if they wish.
- ✔ *Direct Stock Plans,* or DSPs, allow anyone to buy shares directly from the company rather than buying shares on the market.

If you have your eye on a particular company and want to know if it has a DRIP or DSP, you can usually find out online by going to the firm's Web site, following an <u>Investor Relations</u> link, and browsing the contents.

Direct purchase plans are a good way to invest in stocks if you want to start small and build up your shares with regular purchases in the same dollar amount (called *dollar-cost averaging*). Many direct plans automatically withdraw money from your account, and in some, you can start with as little as $50.

You can find out more about DSPs and DRIPs at a soup-to-nuts Web site, Drip Central (`www.dripcentral.com`).

Researching DRIPs and DSPs

If you want to research DSP and DRIP stocks, Netstock Direct (`www.netstockdirect.com`) is the place to go. Netstock Direct is a clearinghouse for direct-purchase data and enrollment links. You can search for stock plans by category, industry, and features such as IRA availability, transaction fees, and minimum purchase amounts. And if a plan has online signup, you can get there from here.

Netstock Direct requires a free registration for its full range of services. See the Register Now link for more information.

Browsing the Netstock Direct home page gives you several possibilities for research.

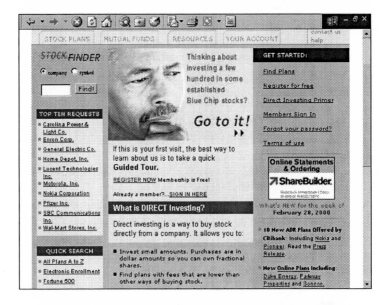

✔ If you have a company already in mind, you can find out about its direct purchase plan (if it has one) by typing the name or symbol in the Stockfinder search box and clicking the Find button.

✔ You can click the links in the Top Ten Requests or Quick Search sections.

✔ The Direct Investing Primer link in the Get Started section is a good place to find out more about this method of owning stock.

To screen stock DRIP and DSP plans according to your chosen criteria, do the following:

1. From the Netstock Direct home page, click the Stock Plans tab.

A stockscreen page appears.

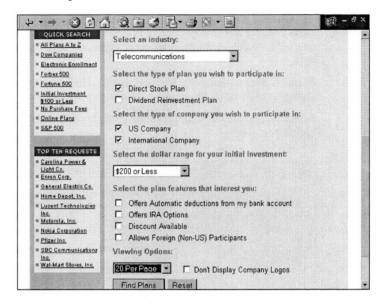

2. Go through the stock screen and select the desired items from the various drop-down lists.

3. Check the appropriate checkboxes for any features that you want the stock screen to look for.

   Remember: You can check more than one checkbox on this page.

4. Click the Find Plans button.

   The following figures show results of a search for telecommunications companies offering DSPs with an investment minimum of $200 or less.

   Links on the search results page take you to plan details and online enrollment. Go to the summary to see the plan's requirements and fees.

Buying registered shares

Dividend Reinvestment Plans (DRIPs) require you to own at least one share of the stock registered in your name. Normally, stocks you buy and sell through a broker are held in the broker's name — called the *street name*. Brokers will register shares for you, but don't be surprised if they charge a fee (look at the broker's Web site under fees for "non-trading services").

If you want to skip your broker entirely, check out First Share, at www.firstshare.com. This is a cooperative in which members trade registered shares they already own in order to help one another start DRIP accounts.

Recordkeeping at Brokerage Sites

There's still a place for paper in online trading. Brokers still send you trade confirmations and account statements for your records. But if your broker gives you a paperless option, such as e-mail statements, you might want to consider it for the convenience.

Just make sure you don't lose those trade confirmations. They're hard evidence, for tax purposes, of your holding period and cost basis, two key factors in computing taxes on capital gains. *See also* Part XII for more on taxes.

Confirmations and settlement

For every purchase or sale at your broker, you get a separate trade confirmation by paper or online, which tells you the exact cost of a purchase or proceeds of a sale.

On a trade confirmation, you find two dates: the date of the trade itself and the date of the *settlement*. The latter, called T+3, is the third business day after the trade. It's the payment deadline for any purchase of securities. If you already had enough cash in your account to cover the trade, you needn't worry — the money is automatically paid.

 The confirmation statement is your last chance to spot any errors and get them corrected. You may have just a couple of days to do this. For details, read the terms and conditions that come with the statement.

Transaction histories

Online trading sites give you the ability to call up a quick record of transactions. This is no substitute for keeping your own records on a desktop finance program, such as Quicken, or in paper files, but it's good for checking recent trades if you're updating your records.

Look for a <u>History</u> link at the page where you get your account balances. (*See also* "Account balance and buying power" in this part.)

You can easily get a customized report or trading summary:

- ✔ At the Charles Schwab site (www.schwab.com), create a customized report by clicking Accounts and then History.

✔ At E*Trade, get a ready-made trade summary by logging in and then clicking the Account Services menu tab and then Account Activity. To get a report that you can customize, log in and then click Portfolios and then Trading History.

Portfolio tracking

If you have all your investments at one online broker firm, you might be able to use the site to track your portfolio and its performance. However, if you have accounts with multiple brokerages, you need to use an all-purpose financial Web site such as MSN Investor or use a desktop program such as Quicken and Microsoft Money.

The tracking tools at your online broker may be worth using if they have automatic updates (that is, you don't have to enter trades) and if they give you one-step convenience.

See also Part X for more on Web-based portfolio-tracking tools.

Setting Up Online Accounts

At the typical e-brokerage, you can complete most of a new-account application online. Some firms even let you apply online from start to finish in a fully paperless process. Others have you print out, sign, and mail a form to complete the application. Your brokerage may not require you to send cash right away, though you must have cash in your trading account when you actually start trading.

The following sections detail application processes, including typical steps you go through and questions you can expect to be asked.

Mail-in applications

Applications for brokerage accounts ask a standard set of questions. Some cover the personal basics: who you are, where do you live, what kind of account you want to set up. Others ask about your assets and investing experience to determine whether higher-risk activity, such as margin trading, is right for you. Expect extra questions if you want to trade options.

To set up a brokerage account that requires you to mail in a printed signature form, visit E*TRADE (www.etrade.com) and follow these steps:

1. From the homepage, click Open an Account.

A new page asks you to choose how you want to apply:

- Choosing Mail Application takes you through an all-paper application process.

- Choosing Apply Online takes you through an application process that combines online and mail-in components.

2. Click Apply Online.

   A screen asks you what type of account you want to set up. *Remember:*

   - Individual and joint accounts are taxable.

   - Traditional, rollover, or Roth IRAs are tax-deferred.

   - The tax status of a custodial account depends on the amount of income it generates and the age of the child.

   Get some expert advice and make sure you understand what these choices mean for you.

3. Some accounts, such as trusts and retirement plans for the self-employed, require mail applications. Check the link Other - Request an Account Kit by Mail to see if the one you want requires a mail application.

4. Choose an account type and click Continue.

5. On the next page, state how you're investment will be paid for and click Continue. Your options include:

   - **Cash:** A cash account is the most restricted. You can only buy securities with money on hand. IRAs and custodial accounts must be cash accounts.

   - **Margin:** In a margin account, you can borrow money from your broker to buy securities, or sell short (that is, sell borrowed securities that you buy back later and return to your broker).

   - **Margin with options trading:** Margin accounts with options trading are considered the most risky and the least suitable for beginning investors.

6. Fill out a series of screens that ask your name and address, phone number, Social Security number, birth date, and country of citizenship. Click Continue after completing each of these screens.

   Prepare to be asked whether you work for a registered broker or dealer. Also, you have to state whether you're an insider — a high-level executive, 10 percent owner, or director of a publicly traded company.

7. Answer a series of questions about your income, net worth, investing goals, and investing experience and click Continue after each question.

These questions help gauge your suitability for higher-risk investments.

When the site asks you to "describe your investment objectives," you're actually telling the brokerage how much risk you're willing to take on. Check the Help link to see how E*Trade defines any terms that may confuse you. *See also* Part I for more on personal risk-assessment.

8. Select where you want your money placed when it is not invested in stocks, funds, bonds, or other securities and click Continue.

Your options include:

- **Money market funds,** which invest in short-term debt from corporations and government. These are a popular parking lot.

- **Tax-exempt portfolios.** These invest in municipal debt — state and local government bonds with interest that is free from federal taxes (and state taxes in the state where they're issued). These portfolios may be right for you if you have a taxable account and you're in a high income-tax bracket.

9. If you're applying to trade options or if you're funding the account with a transfer (as in a rollover from a 401k to an IRA), you have additional questions to answer. Click Continue as you complete each screen.

If you plan to trade options, the site asks you more questions about your investing experience.

When transferring funds, be sure to have a statement handy for the account you're transferring from.

10. Review and/or print out the application for signing and mailing.

All-online applications

Some online brokerages let you go through the entire application process online. For an example of this type of application process, go to DLJ Direct at www.dljdirect.com and then do the following:

Note: You can also apply for a DLJ Direct account by mail or by downloading an application, printing it out, and mailing it in.

1. From the home page, click Apply Online.

The resulting page gives you three account choices: individual, joint, and custodial.

2. Choose one of the account options.

   A new page asks for personal and financial data.

3. Fill out all the requested information.

   You're asked to decide on a user name for online trading.

4. Click Continue at the bottom of the application.

   A customer agreement page appears. This page includes standard terms by which you agree to settle disputes with the broker through arbitration rather than lawsuits.

5. If you want to proceed, click the I Agree button and follow any further instructions to activate your account.

Trading after Hours

You can place online buy and sell orders any time, day or night. But unless you specify otherwise, you order won't be executed until the opening of the next regular trading session (9:30 a.m. to 4 p.m. Eastern) on the Nasdaq Stock Market and New York Stock Exchange.

In a true after-hours trade, buyers and sellers place orders, through brokers, in off-exchange trading systems called electronic communications networks (ECNs). Online brokers enable you to place orders with ECNs as quickly as you can with the big stock markets. But ECNs differ from those markets in ways that tend not to favor the small investor:

- ✔ ECNs lack the middlemen who manage trades and keep bid and ask prices close in the major markets.

- ✔ ECNS have no composite pricing system. Traders in one ECN can't see what they might pay in others and so they may not get the best price.

In light of these risks, online brokers such as E*TRADE and Charles Schwab ask you to read and accept special agreements before making an after-hours trade. As of the writing, they put special restrictions on orders:

- ✔ Only limit orders are allowed.

- ✔ E*TRADE doesn't allow short sales (although Schwab, at this writing, does).

- ✔ E*TRADE requires orders to be in round lots of shares (that is, in numbers divisible by 100).

Check with your own brokerage for its set of rules.

Also, make sure that you make after-hours trades on the correct page. For example:

- ✔ At E*TRADE, click <u>After Hours Trading </u>on the home page.
- ✔ At Schwab, click the Trade tab and then click After Hours (not Stocks).

The trading grid for after-hour trades looks much like the one for regular trades, except that you have fewer choices

Remember: All after-hours trades expire with the end of the session. They don't carry over into the next regular trading session.

Knowing When to Buy and Sell

Successful investing means not only buying the right stocks, but buying and selling them at the right time. This part shows you how you can use online data and news sources to spot stocks on the move — either up and down — and to make buy and sell decisions.

In this part . . .

Assessing Stock Price Movement

You don't need an MBA to grasp the basic principle behind the price moves in a stock — the ups and downs are nothing more than shifting expectations. As MSN Investor states succinctly: "Stock prices change when investors alter their opinion about a company's prospects."

As an investor, you need to look for events, or *catalysts,* that will change the other investors' opinions of a stock. Catalysts include:

✔ Company announcements and news

✔ Analysts' coverage of the stock

✔ Insider trading action

✔ The stock's own price action

Stock news at MSN Investor

MSN Investor is just one of the myriad online sources of opinion on stocks and the market. It's a good place to get the most recent and relevant news about a stock.

Here's how to view the catalysts for a particular stock:

1. At the MSN Investor home page (`moneycentral.msn.com/investor`), click Stocks on the menu bar.

2. Click Research Wizard in the left-hand menu.

3. Type a trading symbol in the Name or Symbol text box, or use the Find button to locate a symbol.

4. Click Go.

   A screen appears showing the selected company's fundamentals — history of sales, earnings, and other information. *See also* Part III for more on company fundamentals.

5. Click Catalysts in the left-hand menu.

   A screen appears with links to news, SEC filings, insider trade data, and MSN's own Advisor FYI alerts.

6. Click <u>View FYI Advisor Alerts</u> for the stock you're researching.

   A screen appears that shows events (with dates) that could move a stock price.

7. Click <u>Description</u> in the right-hand column for an explanation of the event.

Stock news at Bloomberg.com

Bloomberg.com also offers a handy list of stocks making news.

1. Go to the home page at www.Bloomberg.com.

2. Click <u>Stocks on the Move</u> in the Markets section.

A list of "market movers" appears, each with a quote, a small chart, and a brief news story.

Earnings Surprises

When all is said and done, it's profit — more precisely, profit expectations — that drives stock prices. Investors will pay for shares based on what they think a company will make for them as owners. That's why earnings reports are so closely watched, and why stocks that earn more than the experts expected are often rewarded with big price hikes.

Online financial portals do daily reports on these surprise earnings, both positive and negative. They also list the stocks that hit their earnings targets. Checking these lists is a good way to screen for stocks that are likely to draw increased investor attention.

You might use the list of upside-surprise stocks as a starting point for further research into the companies, if you're not following them already.

Remember: The best time to screen for earnings surprises is when earnings are being reported. Months at the end of calendar quarters (April, July, October, and January) see the heaviest volume of reports, usually from the second week of the month onward.

Screening for surprises at Yahoo! Finance

To get a current list of earnings surprises at Yahoo! Finance:

1. Go to the home page at quote.yahoo.com.

2. Click the <u>Surprises</u> link after Earnings in the Yahoo! Finance table of contents.

A page appears that shows both upside and downside surprises, with details on the reported and expected earnings per share (EPS).

Today's Earnings - As of 2:52 pm ET 6-Mar-00

Extreme Surprises | High Revenue | A-C | D-F | G-I | J-L | M-O | P-R | S-U | V-X | Y-Z

Upside Surprises*

Ticker	Company Name	Qtr Revenues	Net Income	Expected EPS	Reported EPS	% Surprise	More Info
AMCV	AMER CLASSIC	55.49M	33000	-0.01	0.00	100.00	Chart, News, SEC, Msge Profile, Research, Insider
KM	K MART CORP	11.11B	412.00M	0.69	0.77	11.59	Chart, News, SEC, Msge Profile, Research, Insider
BHI	BAKER-HUGHES	1.10B	-92.80M	-0.03	-0.03	0.00	Chart, News, SEC, Msge Profile, Research, Insider

Downside Surprises*

Ticker	Company Name	Qtr Revenues	Net Income	Expected EPS	Reported EPS	% Surprise	More Info
UNFI	UTD NATURAL FDS	231.40M	-4.53M	-0.05	-0.07	-40.00	Chart, News, SEC, Ms Profile, Research, Insi

For more in-depth analysis covering over 6,000 equities, a free trial to Zacks premium services is

3. Click a ticker symbol to get a detailed quote.

4. Click any of the links in the More Info section to get charts, profiles, and other research.

If the list of surprises is long, use the links above the table to focus on categories alphabetically or by dollar amount.

Screening for surprises at CBS MarketWatch

CBS MarketWatch also includes information on earnings surprises, including daily tables and news articles. Do the following:

1. Go to the home page at cbs.marketwatch.com.

2. Click the Regular Features link in the Find Your News section.

3. Click the Earnings Surprises link in the Newswatch section.

4. To see a daily table, click Market Data.

5. Click the Surprises link in the Earnings section.

Screening for surprises at ClearStation

At ClearStation, you can call up a list of the day's earnings surprises and rank them by several criteria, including the percentage size of the surprise, change in volume, and change in price:

1. Go to the ClearStation home page at www.clearstation.com.

2. Click Earnings Surprises just under the horizontal bar that reads Welcome to ClearStation.

In the screen shown here, the stocks are ranked by the day's trading volume in descending order.

Earnings Surprise : all exchanges (1-13 of 13) sorted by **Volume** in descending order

Symbol	Last	Change	%Change	High	Low	Volume ▼	Vol % Change	Earnings Consensus	Earnings Actual	% Surpris
HRC	5.00	-0.69	-12.09%	5.81	4.94	3,363,000	108.14%	0.16	0.16	0.00%
DSGX	66.75	3.50	5.53%	70.00	65.62	752,300	196.50%	-0.06	-0.09	-50.00%
FRAG	8.75	0.62	7.69%	8.94	8.62	204,700	-13.75%	0.26	0.27	3.85%
EMBX	19.25	1.38	7.69%	19.62	18.00	136,300	301.08%	0.18	0.20	11.11%
MANC	8.19	-0.47	-5.42%	9.12	7.56	125,500	118.46%	N/A	0.10	N/A
EIM	33.25	-0.25	-0.75%	36.50	33.00	82,300	154.98%	-0.21	-0.16	23.81%
NRI	5.25	-0.06	-1.13%	5.38	5.19	62,800	-39.44%	0.15	0.15	0.00%
KLU	5.50	0.00	0.00%	5.69	5.31	56,900	-74.07%	-0.19	-0.20	-5.26%
DGTC	7.75	0.12	1.64%	8.12	7.50	37,800	-15.26%	0.21	0.22	4.76%
RDL	3.00	0.00	0.00%	3.12	3.00	18,000	228.31%	N/A	-0.95	N/A
SRS	1.62	0.00	0.00%	1.75	1.62	10,200	-85.52%	N/A	-0.23	N/A
FRED	15.19	0.19	1.25%	15.50	15.06	8,800	-83.46%	0.31	0.32	3.23%
HST	5.88	0.00	0.00%	5.88	5.88	0	-65.59%	N/A	-4.09	N/A

Graphs: Graphs: Return to
One by One In Bulk   Front Door

Community Message Preview for stocks in this List

Symbol	Start of Message	Date
HRC	Might be at its bottom but don't see any significant upward activity for	Mar 7 2000 10:04AM

3. Click any links at the top of the columns to rank the stocks by that category.

Clicking a column link again reverses the order.

Sometimes Wall Street's reaction to an earnings surprise seems completely contrary — as when a downside surprise touches off a rally of high volume trading. To find out what's going on, click the trading symbol link to call up a page of charts, discussion, and news headlines to find some clues.

Earnings warnings

Some warning signs related to earnings that you can be on the watch for include:

✓ **Pre-announcements:** Companies tend to announce bad news, if they have it, in so-called *pre-announcements*. Keep an eye out for pre-announcements about a month before the time of earnings reports. Bad news may be a signal to sell, or it may be indicate a buying opportunity if the stock market overreacts to a short-term problem.

✔ **Future quarters:** A future quarters warning can come in the fine print of quarterly reports or in the company's statements to analysts in the conference call that often occurs when the report is released.

You check out a list of recent earnings warnings at CNNfn:

1. Go to www.cnnfn.com.

2. Click <u>Investor Research Center</u> under the Markets heading.

3. Click the Earnings Warnings tab.

   A list of the most recent warnings appears.

4. Click <u>More</u> under that short list.

   A table of earnings pre-announcements appears. The table shows the date of the announcement, the name and ticker of the company, and the earnings period covered.

5. Check out the analysts' consensus versus the per-share earnings forecast by the company.

   The difference between the two shows how drastic the revision was.

6. To find out what happened to the company's stock price in the wake of the announcement, click a trading symbol for a quote.

7. From here, you can call up a chart or profile on the company.

 Earnings warnings show up in the news headlines of finance portals. To watch for the warnings on a stock you're tracking, you can use news-alert programs. ***See also*** "Triggering News and Price Alerts" in this part for more information.

Industry Trends

A change in the outlook for an industry, such as semiconductors or banking, can drive stock prices up or down sharply — even without significant news from individual companies themselves. Wall Street assumes that leading firms in an industry will rise and fall with the industry's fortunes.

Watching industry trends at CBS MarketWatch

If you want to buy stocks when expectations are rising for an industry, you need to know which industries are currently leading the market. You can identify the leading industries at CBS MarketWatch.

For a quick snapshot of hot industries, follow these steps:

1. At the CBS MarketWatch home page (cbs.marketwatch.com), click Market Data at the top of the screen.

2. Under Research in the table of contents, click Industry Analysis.

A page appears showing the top 10 and bottom 10 performing Dow Jones industry indexes over a recent time period (such as three months).

3. To change the time period, select from the pull-down menu above and to the right of the top-10 lists.

You can choose from as short as one week to as long as five years.

Check whether an industry is on the one-week top 10 but not on longer-term leader lists. That may mean Wall Street is just now starting to recognize its improved prospects.

4. If you want to find out how stocks within a given industry group have performed, click an industry name.

A page showing the top 10 and bottom 10 stocks appears. You can also click a chart icon in the right-hand column to call up a chart.

5. Click Industry Analyzer to get small charts of every company in the group.

For more in-depth analysis of industry trends and interactive charts, you can use CBS MarketWatch to get market data. Follow these steps:

1. Go to the CBS MarketWatch home page (cbs.marketwatch.com).

2. Click Market Data.

3. Click Industry Indexes under Indexes, Misc. in the Stocks column.

A table appears showing current prices for dozens of industry indexes, including indexes from different sources for the same industries.

By clicking an index name, you can see current quotes for the individual stocks that comprise it.

4. Click a symbol in the Sym. column to start interactive charting.

5. On the quote page that appears next, click Interactive Charting.

A simple chart (price only, no volume) for the index appears.

6. Click <u>Show All Controls</u> in the shaded menu at the left.

   Doing so opens a column of pull-down menus that allow you to adjust the chart's time-frame, style, and indicators, as well as add other indexes or stocks for comparison.

7. If you want a new time frame, select one from the first pull-down menu.

8. To compare an index to a stock, another industry index, or a market index, use the boxes under <u>Compare To</u> and click the link <u>Compare To</u> after you make your selections.

Courtesy of CBS MarketWatch

Charting two indexes gives you a clear picture of how dramatically market leadership can shift from one industry to another.

Watching industry trends at Bloomberg.com

For a quick look at industry groups making sharp up or down moves in current trading, use Bloomberg.com:

1. Go to the Bloomberg.com home page (www.bloomberg.com).

2. Click the Markets icon.

3. Click <u>Industry Movers</u> in the Stocks section.

Watching industry trends at Yahoo!

At Yahoo! Finance, you can sort the financial news by industry:

1. Go to the home page at `quote.yahoo.com`.

2. Click <u>By Industry</u> under the Financial News heading in the table of contents.

3. Click the main headings or sub-headings to see the sorted news headlines.

4. Click the ellipses (...) after some of the lists to bring up more sub-headings.

Market Trends

Following the market's day-to-day behavior is a snap online.

Making intelligent predictions about the market's future direction requires you to know something about the economic factors that drive the major index like the Standard & Poor's 500.

Federal Reserve news

The Federal Reserve directly affects stock prices by manipulating interest rates, and Wall Street watches it like a hawk. To see what the Fed has been doing and saying:

1. Go to the Bloomberg home page (`www.Bloomberg.com`).

2. Click <u>Markets</u> on the menu bar and then click <u>Fed Watch.</u>

   A page appears with links to articles and audio archives of Fed officials' testimony and speeches. (You'll need to download RealPlayer, from `www.real.com`, to play the audio.)

Economic news

Bloomberg carries reports on economic indicators, both in the U.S. and abroad, on its Economies page. At the home page (`www.bloomberg.com`), click the Markets icon and then click <u>Economies</u>.

To see what economic reports are scheduled in the coming days — and what the experts expect from them — go to the Economic Calendar at CNNfn:

1. At the home page (`cnnfn.com`), click <u>Investor Research Center</u>.

2. Click the Economic Calendar tab for a schedule of upcoming data releases compiled by Briefing.com.

You see "consensus" estimates — such as the consumer price index analysts expect to see in the next inflation report. Briefing.com's own estimates also appear here, along with data from previous reports.

If you just can't get enough economic data, visit the Dismal Scientist (www.dismal.com). Click <u>Toolkit</u> to see what the site offers in addition to economic news and data.

Technical indicators

As with individual stocks, technical analysis of the market has produced a vast array of tools. All aim, in some fashion, to identify price and volume patterns that have some value in predicting future market action.

Such information is generally not free online. But you can get quite a lot of free information at one site, the charting service Decision Point:

1. Go to www.decisionpoint.com.

2. Click any of the Free or Sample areas.

    Go to Daily Charts and Reports, for instance, and then click the <u>Click Here to See Sample Area</u> link for a list of market indexes and indicators.

Decision Point offers subscriptions to its Web site service, including the daily charts and a technical analysis course. *See also* "Price/Volume Signals" in this part for technical charting of individual stocks.

Sentiment indicators

When advisors and investors go to extremes of optimism or pessimism, many experts believe the market may be about to turn the other way. Subscribers to the Wall Street Journal (WSJ) and Barron's online can get a weekly sentiment scorecard at the Barron's Market Lab (these online editions cost $29 a year for the WSJ or Barron's print subscribers, $59 for non-subscribers). Visit the Barron's home page (www.barrons.com) to subscribe or sign up for a free trial.

Price/Volume Signals

Stock analysis generally falls into two categories:

  ✔ **Technical analysis** of stocks seeks to predict prices by studying patterns of price and volume action.

✔ **Fundamental analysis** looks at the performance of the underlying business.

Both categories are important to buying and selling decisions. For an overview of the fundamental side, see Part III. For a look at online technical tools, read on.

Trend-spotting at ClearStation

ClearStation combines technical charting with an online community and the usual investor-site features, such as quotes and news. Also, its extensive tutorial section explains many price and volume patterns and shows how they look on charts.

To sample the site:

1. Go to the home page, www.clearstation.com.

2. Click the Education button for the tutorial.

The tutorial offers sections on trading basics, such as understanding trends and other patterns.

3. Click the Tag & Bag button to call up an "A-list" of stocks that are going through notable events.

4. Click the trading symbol for any stock in the list to call up a chart.

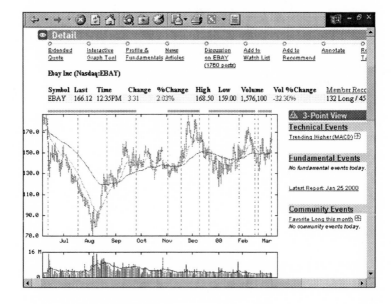

Charts show two moving averages (a "fast" 12-day and a "slow" 26-day line). The darker line is the slow average. Horizontal bars at the top of the chart show up or down trends by color — pink for down, green for up. A daily volume chart just below the price chart shows volume on up and down days by blue and red bars.

ClearStation members (registration is free) can customize charts for different periods and sizes. They can also set up watch lists to follow and participate in the bulletin boards. Click the Join Now! button on the home page to sign up.

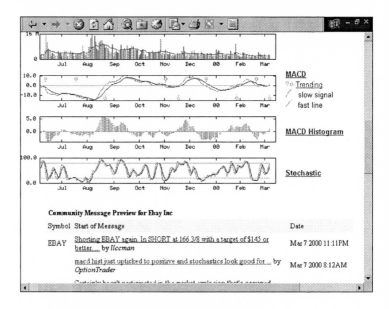

5. Scroll down the chart page to a set of horizontal graphs that shows key technical indicators. They are:

• **MACD (Moving Average Convergence-Divergence):** This shows acceleration of price movements, either up or down. When the "fast" (12-day) moving average crosses the "slow" (26-day) average going up, that may signal a new up trend. Up and down trends are marked by pointers above or below the MACD lines.

• **MACD Histogram:** This shows how wide the divergence is at any point between the fast and slow lines. Click the link to the right of the chart for some tips on reading these curves.

- **Stochastic.** This is a measure of how far a stock is deviating from the middle of its recent trading range. High and low swings on the curve suggest points where the stock may be unsustainably high or low ("overbought" or "oversold") and ready for a snap back to the middle of its range.

You also can call up any of the preceding charts for a stock at ClearStation by typing the trading symbol in the Enter Symbol box on the home page and clicking the Get Graphs! button.

Spotting price breakouts and other signals

A *breakout price* is a new price high with a difference — the stock has passed through a previous high set some time earlier. Many experts see this as a significant technical event, especially if it comes on higher-than-average volume.

Breakouts are hard to spot in quotes but easy to see in charts:

1. Go to the ClearStation home page (`www.clearstation.com`).

2. Click the Tag & Bag button to see the "A-List" stocks.

3. Click Technical Events to see a full list of stocks in record price breakouts and other significant patterns.

In each category (such as Record Price Break Out, Record Volume, and so on), columns show how many stocks in each stock exchange or market are undergoing a particular event.

4. Click the number for any category to see a list of the stocks with current prices and volumes.

The BB column is not a stock exchange, but rather a bulletin board for buying and selling small, infrequently traded stocks that don't meet the requirements for NASDAQ's national market. These stocks are highly speculative issues.

Custom charting at ASK Research

For technicians who want to construct their own charts using a wide range of sophisticated tools, ASK Research has an easy-to-use (and free) interactive site:

1. Go to `www.askresearch.com`.

2. Click <u>Daily Charts</u> or <u>Intraday Charts</u> (the latter for the shortest time frame).

A grid appears.

3. Use the pull-down menus to select a stock (by symbol), the time frame, type of price marker (such as bar or line), up to three moving averages, and Bollinger bands, if you want those indicators.

   The technical indicators will be shown below the main price chart.

   Click the links for explanations of the indicators. Click the <u>Instructions</u> link at the bottom of the screen if you need more help.

4. Click the Create Chart button after you're finished.

Triggering News and Price Alerts

Many financial sites and online brokers offer some form of messaging, either by e-mail or on the Web, to alert you to events that may be signals to buy or sell a stock.

For a stock you own, alerts can be an early warning system that saves you having to watch prices constantly. You can program alerts to tell you whether a stock in your portfolio has taken a sudden dive. That may not be a signal to sell, but it should lead you to check the news on the stock to see what caused the dip.

Alerts are often linked to stock portfolios (or stock watch lists that you don't own). Part X describes how to set up portfolios and other stock lists.

Setting up alerts at Quicken.com

If you keep any portfolio or watch list at Quicken.com, the site automatically notifies you of alerts on your stocks when you go to the home page (`www.quicken.com`). Quicken.com price alerts notify you of analyst upgrades and downgrades, split announcements, and price and volume events.

To utilize alert and portfolio services, Quicken.com requires free registration. Sign up and sign on (follow the instructions at the home page) and then do the following to customize your alert settings:

1. Go to the home page (`www.quicken.com`).

2. Check for any alerts by clicking any of the red buttons next to the stock symbols in the Mini-Portfolio column.

3. To view or change alert settings, click the Investing tab.

4. Click Alerts on the horizontal menu bar.

   A list of alerts for your portfolio and watch-list stocks appears.

5. Click the Change button to see the settings.

6. Put check marks next to items that you want to be alerted about.

   On this screen, you can also ask Quicken.com to use a special pop-up window on the home page to signal new alerts.

7. In volume and price boxes in the Stock Performance section, specify the minimum percentage change in price and volume that will set off an alert on any of your stocks.

   If you're not getting any price and volume alerts, Quicken will advise you to make the thresholds lower.

8. Click the Save Changes button after you're finished.

Setting up price alerts at MSN

MSN Investor has a downloadable program called News Alert that flashes an alert signal in your Windows taskbar when you're online. News Alert covers the universe of online topics, from stocks to sports, and uses content from MSNBC.

You can customize the stock-related information from MSN by following these steps:

1. Go to `msnbc.com /toolkit.asp`.

2. Click the News Alert bulls-eye symbol, or click <u>News Alert</u> in the Cooltools section.

3. Click the <u>Download Tool for Windows 95, 98 or NT</u> link.

4. Follow the download and setup instructions.

   After you start the News Alert program, watch for a flashing bulls-eye in your taskbar. Click it to open a window showing the latest news.

5. After the tool download is complete, click Customize at the top of the alert window.

   A Personal Stocks page appears.

Customize MSN MoneyCentral Investor Stocks

PERSONAL STOCKS

Type the symbols for the stocks you track below. You can request alerts when your stock changes by more than a specified percentage in a single day, when your stock rises to or above a specific price, and/or when your stock falls to or below a certain level.

If you're not sure of the correct symbol for a particular stock, you can find a company symbol at MSN MoneyCentral Investor.

If you want to stop receiving alerts for a stock, just delete the symbol below.

Symbol	changes by	%, rises to $	, or falls to $
tstn	5		135
cmrc	5	260	
orcl	5	85	
msft	5		90
csco	5	145	125

_6._ Type symbols for the stocks you want to follow, along with price levels for alerts.

You can specify percentage changes as well as specific prices.

Below the table is a box you can check if you want to get a summary of your stocks each weekday when the market closes.

_7._ After you're done, click Save.

TIP

Price alerts are a way to set buy and sell levels for a stock. Another method — one that makes the transaction automatic — is to place limit or stop orders with a broker. **_See also_** Part V.

Setting up price alerts at Yahoo!

Yahoo! offers stock alerts as part of its Messenger feature, which also includes instant messaging, voice chat, news, and sports scores. Yahoo! Messenger can track stocks that you include in your portfolio. **_See also_** Part X on setting up stock portfolios.

Download the Messenger program by clicking Messenger at the Yahoo! front page (www.yahoo.com) or clicking Instant Stock Alerts just below the table of contents at Yahoo! Finance (finance.yahoo.com).

Part VII

IPOs

Initial public offerings — *IPOs* — are a boon to investors who want to research companies in depth. IPOs require plenty of disclosure about a firm's past record, present structure, and future prospects. Virtually all of this information finds its way onto the Internet. With some luck, as an online investor, you can participate in some of these offerings. The following sections describe both sides of the IPO process — research and investing.

In this part . . .

Buying IPOs Online

Small investors used to have no hope of getting hot IPOs at the offering price, but the Internet has changed that. Some online brokers give account holders a chance to participate in offerings. A handful even allow the true small fry, with account balances in the low four figures, to join in.

Money still talks, of course. Big institutional investors such as mutual funds continue to receive preferred treatment in the allotting of IPO shares, as do the wealthy individual investors. Small investors get what's left over, and that may not be much.

On the other hand, there's really no downside to submitting an offer with your broker to see whether you'll be one of the lucky investors who gets in on a hot IPO (or just a warm one).

IPOs are risky investments, though you can't deny that some have done extremely well in recent years. For a skeptical view of IPOs as an investment vehicle for ordinary folks, see UCLA professor Ivo Welch's article "Investing in IPOs for Small Retail Investors" at `www.iporesources.org/ipoinvesting.html`.

IPO Brokers

To see a list of online brokers who offer IPO participation, go to Gomez Advisors (`www.gomez.com` or `www.gomezadvisors.com`) and follow these steps:

1. Click Brokers under Choose a Channel.

2. Click The IPO Process in the Gomez Resources column.

3. Click Who Offers Access to IPOs? in the section, Which Internet Broker Should I Choose?

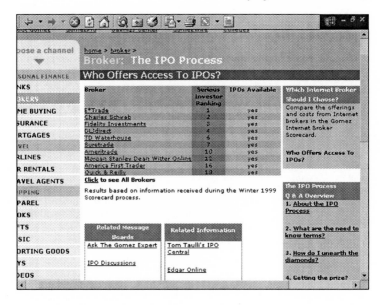

ose a channel   home > broker >

Broker: The IPO Process

Who Offers Access To IPOs?

NKS
)KERS
ME BUYING
SURANCE
RTGAGES
VE.
RLINES
R RENTALS
AVEL AGENTS
PPING
PAREL
OKS
-TS
SIC
ORTING GOODS
YS
)EOS

Broker	Serious Investor Ranking	IPOs Available	Which Internet Broker Should I Choose?
E*Trade	1	yes	Compare the offerings and costs from Internet Brokers in the Gomez Internet Broker Scorecard.
Charles Schwab	2	yes	
Fidelity Investments	3	yes	
DLJdirect	4	yes	
TD Waterhouse	6	yes	
Suretrade	7	yes	
Ameritrade	10	yes	Who Offers Access To IPOs?
Morgan Stanley Dean Witter Online	12	yes	
America First Trader	16	yes	
Quick & Reilly	18	yes	

Click to see All Brokers

Results based on information received during the Winter 1999 Scorecard process.

The IPO Process
Q & A Overview

1. **About the IPO Process**

Related Message Boards	Related Information
Ask The Gomez Expert	Tom Taulli's IPO Central
IPO Discussions	Edgar Online

2. **What are the need to know terms?**

3. **How do I unearth the diamonds?**

4. **Getting the prize?**

4. Click any of the broker names on the list.

Gomez's table of overall rankings appears.

5. Click review next to a broker name on that table for details on its services.

In addition to the large online brokers (such as E*TRADE and DLJdirect) that offer IPO participation, a few investment firms have made a specialty out of online IPOs. Three worth noting are

✔ Wit Capital (www.witcapital.com)

✔ W.R. Hambrecht & Co.'s OpenIPO (www.openipo.com)

✔ MercerPartners IPO Syndicate (www.iposyndicate.com)

All three firms have fairly low minimums for opening accounts (between $2,000 and $4,000).

Some online brokers offer IPO participation only to customers that have sizable accounts, with minimums of $100,000 or $500,000. As with other high-risk investments, you can also expect to fill out a questionnaire to gauge your suitability for IPOs, which are not appropriate for investors who need safety and investment income.

Discovering the Offering Process

The exact rules for IPO participants vary a bit from broker to broker (*see* "Flipping" in this part), but at all brokers, the offering process hinges on several key events:

- ✔ **Notification.** A broker announces (either on the Web page or via e-mail) that shares of a new issue are available. Qualified customers can submit offers within a certain period of time (sometimes just a couple of hours) and download a preliminary prospectus.

- ✔ **Conditional offers** (also called "indications of interest"). Customers tell the broker how many shares they are willing to buy. At this point, the issuing company has set a proposed price range for its shares, but this can later change. Conditional offers are not firm buy orders — they can be taken back at any time before the offering is priced.

- ✔ **Pricing and Reconfirmation.** The SEC declares the stock offering effective and the final share price is announced. At this point — usually the day before the stock trades for the first time — investors are asked to reconfirm their conditional offers.

The time window for reconfirming can be quite short — a couple of hours in the evening, for example — and missing the deadline scuttles your offer.

- ✔ **Allocation.** On the first trading day, the broker allocates the available shares to online participants at the offering price. Whether the customers actually get shares depends on how many the broker received, how strong the demand is, and what policies the broker has established for distributing shares when there aren't enough to go around. Each broker has particular rules for this, spelled out in the IPO section of its Web site.

Offerings from Wit Capital

Wit Capital describes the rules of its IPO process, such as the guidelines it follows for allocating shares, in a guide that is open to visitors as well as customers.

1. Go to the home page at www.witcapital.com.

2. Click IPOs and Other Offerings.

3. Under IPO Tutorial, click Very Simple Guide.

Offerings from E*TRADE

To find out about the offering process at E*TRADE:

1. Go to the home page at www.etrade.com.

2. Click <u>IPOs</u> in the menu under Investing.

   The IPO Center page has current offerings and alerts along with sections devoted to learning and research.

3. Click <u>How to Participate</u> in the IPO Info Desk section.

Offerings from DLJdirect

At the DLJdirect home page (www.dljdirect.com):

1. Click IPO Center.

2. Click <u>The Offering Process at DLJdirect and How to Participate</u>.

3. Scroll down the page and click <u>Qualifying Criteria</u> to find out what you need to participate.

Flipping

To keep the price of a stock from sagging shortly after it starts trading, brokers discourage the practice of *flipping* — selling your allocated shares on the market shortly after you get them. Flipping certainly isn't illegal, but online investors who try it may face some penalty, such as being frozen out of the next IPO they request.

Different brokers define flipping differently: At E*TRADE, *flipping* is trading a stock within 30 days of the pricing, while Wit Capital sets the limit at 60 days. Different brokers also have different ways of deterring flipping. Look in a broker's IPO tutorial or FAQs for details.

Investing in Aftermarket IPOs

IPO investing turns democratic when the shares are publicly traded. At that point, any investor can access them. The problem with some IPOs is that every investor wants them, and their price pokes a new hole in the ozone layer.

The IPO buying frenzy usually settles down after a few days or weeks, which gives patient, research-driven investors time to learn about an IPO's market behavior and its business fundamentals. For hot new stock issues especially, this "aftermarket" trading may be the first real chance for an online investor to own an IPO. ***See also*** "Keeping up with Recent IPOs" for information on how to identify and monitor aftermarket IPOs.

Keeping Up with Recent IPOs

IPOs are quoted and charted just like other stocks once they go public. You can call up price and volume data on them in the usual ways. *See also* Part II.

The Internet also has plenty of sites devoted just to IPOs. You can visit these pages for some focused tracking on companies that have recently gone public. You can see how demand is holding up for a new issue after the IPO hype has faded and independent, critical analysis starts entering the picture.

Hoover's IPO Central

Hoover's IPO Central offers a research package (company capsules with news and financial links) similar to what Hoover's provides for other stocks. *See also* Part III. To track IPO information at Hoover's IPO Central:

1. Go to www.hoovers.com.

2. Click IPO Central.

3. For a list of all companies that have gone public in the past several years, click View IPOs in the IPO Central menu. You can sort the IPOs by industry or by lead underwriter.

4. To see the winners and losers from the most recent quarter — new issues that either rose the highest or fell the farthest from their offer prices — click IPO Scorecard.

CBS MarketWatch

To track aftermarket performance and keep up with the latest IPO news at CBS MarketWatch:

1. Go to cbs.marketwatch.com.

2. Click IPOWatch in the News Sections menu. This takes you to a page of IPO News as well as links to performance data.

3. Click Aftermarket Results under Data in the IPOWatch Contents menu.

4. Click any ticker symbol on the table to go to a full quote, with links to charts, news and fundamental data.

EDGAR Online's IPO Express

To track IPO information at EDGAR Online's IPO Express:

1. Go to www.edgar-online.com/ipoexpress.

2. Click IPO Performance.

   A table appears, listing the return on IPOs over several time spans, from 30 days to a year.

3. Click the top of each column to see stocks ranked for each period.

4. Click ticker symbols for quotes and company names for corporate information.

IPOhome.com

To track IPO information at IPOhome.com:

1. Go to www.ipo-fund.com.

2. Click any of the links under IPO Pricings or IPO Rankings.

   The Foreign link, for instance, lists IPOs of overseas-based firms traded in the U.S.

Renaissance Capital, which runs IPOhome.com, also offers an IPO mutual fund.

1. Click IPO Mutual Fund on the home page to find out more about the IPO+ Aftermarket Fund.

2. To see the fund's favorite stocks among recent IPOs, click Top Holdings.

3. Click Performance to see how the fund has fared against the Russell 2000 index of small stocks. *See also* Part VIII for more on mutual funds.

Monitoring IPO News

Bookmark the sites in this section to stay current on companies that are going public. All of them list the latest IPO filings, expected pricings, and other IPO news.

Along with these general lists of IPOs in the pipeline, your broker can keep a list of IPOs that are available to customers. To see what E*TRADE has on tap, for instance, go to the home page at www.etrade.com and click IPOs.

News at Yahoo! Finance

To check out IPO news at Yahoo! Finance:

1. Go to the home page at <u>finance.yahoo.com</u>.

2. Click <u>IPOs</u> in the table of contents after the U.S. Markets heading.

A page that shows new filings as well as pricings, withdrawals, and other IPO news appears.

3. Click <u>Profile</u> links for data summaries on the companies and the offerings.

News at Hoover's IPO Central

To check out IPO news at Hoover's IPO Central:

1. Go to the Hoover's home page at `www.hoovers.com`.

2. Click IPO Central.

3. Click Latest Filings in the IPO Central menu.

4. Click the company name on this table to go to a brief description of the firm and the offering.

5. Click the link after Industry to see other firms in the company's industry.

Links with a yellow key lead to information (such as real-time SEC filings) for Hoover's subscribers.

6. Click the Back button to return to IPO Central

7. Click Latest Pricings in the IPO Central menu to see a table of IPOs that just started trading.

News at CBS MarketWatch

To check out IPO news at CBS MarketWatch:

1. Go to the front page at `cbs.marketwatch.com`.

2. Click IPOWatch in the News Sections menu.

3. Click <u>Recent Filings</u> under Data in the IPOWatch Contents menu.

4. Click company names on the table to go to Hoover's capsules.

5. Browse the IPOWatch page for other news and commentary.

News briefs give you the main IPO stories of the day, with links to more information.

News at Red Herring

The magazine Red Herring, which specializes in the coverage of up-and-coming technology companies, has plenty of news and data about IPOs at its Web site. To check out IPO news at Red Herring:

1. Go to the home page at `www.redherring.com`.

2. Click IPO News.

   A page of IPO News, commentary and links appears.

3. Click View IPO Calendar.

   You see a table of upcoming pricings as well as links to other IPO data appears.

4. Click Filings just under IPO News to see companies that have just filed to go public.

News at EDGAR Online's IPO Express

To check out IPO news at EDGAR Online's IPO Express:

1. Go to the home page at `www.edgar-online.com/ipoexpress`.

2. Click Latest Filings.

   A short list of new filings is also on the main page under IPO headlines.

News at IPO.com

To check out IPO news at IPO.com:

1. Go to the home page at `www.ipo.com`.

2. Click Filings.

3. Click the company name for a summary of the offering.

Researching IPOs

Until a few weeks after the stock begins trading, your main source of information will be the official filings. News and rating services offer further insight (or at least pass along the current Wall Street buzz). You can also get more in-depth research for a price, either in monthly subscriptions or pay-per-view reports.

S-1s and other SEC filings

When a company decides to offer shares for trading on stock markets, it must file a lengthy disclosure document with the Securities and Exchange Commission. This "registration statement" includes the company history, its products, risk factors and competitive situation, the purpose of the offering, details on ownership, and much more.

For most domestic IPOs, this statement is filed as Form S-1. It is also issued to prospective buyers of the new issue as the preliminary prospectus, or "red herring." Amendments are filed as Form S-1/A.

You can call up S-1s and other filings directly from the SEC through its EDGAR system. *See also* Part III. Or you can get some help in navigating the S-1 document if you go to the site of EDGAR Online, a company that repackages the SEC data into a more accessible form:

1. Go to the home page of EDGAR Online's IPO Express at www.edgar-online.com/ipoexpress.

2. Find an IPO from one of the lists (Recent Filings, Upcoming Pricings, Quiet Period Expiring, and so on).

3. Click a company name to call up a profile.

   The Company Profile: Introduction page has links to the company itself and to material from filings in the SEC's EDGAR system. The links listed below the company's contact information sum up key data from the filings.

4. Click <u>Offering</u> for a summary of the IPO.

   You can click the lead underwriter's name to see what other IPOs the underwriter has been involved in. From there, you can research the outcome of those IPOs to get a sense of the underwriter's track record.

5. Click <u>Financials</u> for the company's latest profit-and-loss data and balance sheet.

   You can see figures for the latest full fiscal year compared to the year before, and figures for the current fiscal year to date also compared to the same period a year earlier.

6. Click the following other links for more information:

   • <u>Mgmt</u> tells who the top executives are and what they get paid.

   • <u>Biz</u> provides details on the company's products and services.

- <u>Shareholders</u> has a list of principal stockholders.

- <u>Competition</u> lists leading business rivals.

If you can't find what you're looking for in the column of links, try using your browser's Find function to look for a word match (on Internet Explorer 5, look in the option under Edit on the menu bar). Try searching for the phrase "Shares Eligible for Future Sale" to get details on an IPO's lock-up period (the period during which insiders cannot sell their shares).

Ratings and commentary

How can you tell the potential moonshots from the duds among upcoming IPOs? Several Web sites offer informed opinions for free, and you can get more in-depth analysis for a fee. Here are some good places for ratings and/or comment:

- **CBS MarketWatch:** For IPO ratings and commentary:

  1. Go to cbs.marketwatch.com.

  2. Click IPOCenter under News Sections.

  3. Click any of the links under News and Commentary or browse the headlines.

- **IPOhome.com:** The site of Renaissance Capital, a research and mutual-fund firm, features an "IPO of the Week" and sells research reports on upcoming IPOs. For commentary:

  1. Go to the home page at www.ipo-fund.com.

  2. Click <u>IPO of the Week</u> under IPO Intelligence.

  3. Click the trading symbol of the featured IPO for a summary report. Click Get a Full IPO Report to buy one ($50) or see a sample.

- **Red Herring:** The online site of Red Herring magazine rates demand for pending IPOs on a five-step scale, from "cool" to "red hot." For commentary:

  1. Go to the home page at www.redherring.com.

  2. Click IPO News.

  3. Click View IPO Calendar.

  The Upcoming Pricings table shows the Street Poll rating for each stock. You can click the names of companies and underwriters to get further background information on the offerings (you can also find this info at www.ipo.com).

✔ **IpoPros.com:** This site, mostly closed to non-paying visitors, offers a free glimpse of its ratings for IPOs just about to start trading. For ratings:

1. Go to the home page at www.ipopros.com.

2. Click The Week Ahead to see which stocks are rated as "Hot!" To get the research behind these ratings, you need to subscribe for $25 a month.

You can get some sense of an IPO's future market direction by watching its final pricing. If an IPO is priced above the range projected in its initial filing, demand for the shares presumably was better than expected. A pricing at the bottom of the range (or lower) sendsthe opposite signal.

Tutorial Sites

To read about the rules, customs, and pitfalls of public offerings, try these tutorial sites:

✔ **E*TRADE (**www.etrade.com): Click IPOs, and then click any of the links listed under IPO Info Desk.

✔ **The Taulli Report (**www.taulli.com): Longtime IPO reporter Tom Taulli has a number of articles at his Web site explaining the IPO process. From the home page, click IPOs and then click any of the links under Understanding IPOs.

✔ **Gomez Advisors (**www.gomez.com): From the home page, click Brokers and then click The IPO Process in the menu under Gomez Resources.

Other sites, such as IPO-Home, CBS MarketWatch, and IPO.com, also have tutorials and glossaries.

Mutual Funds

Online investors have access to thousands of mutual funds, which are as easy as stocks to buy and sell on the Internet. Along with other pooled investment products such as index securities, mutual funds give small investors a way to spread risk across the market and carry out their investment strategies. The following pages show where to research and trade mutual funds on the Web. For investing in bond funds, see Part IX.

In this part . . .

Asset Allocation in Mutual Funds

Asset allocation means dividing your investment dollars among a few broad investment categories, such as bonds, cash (or money-market funds), large-cap domestic stocks, small-cap domestic stocks, and foreign stocks.

The mix you choose depends on your age, income, expected spending needs, risk tolerance, and other factors. ***See also*** Part I. Mutual funds are the simplest way to divide your portfolio into these different investment categories.

Several online financial sites offer help in allocating your investments:

✔ MSN Investor has an Asset Allocator program in the Prepare to Invest section of its home page. You can get an allocation formula simply by plugging in a desired rate of return.

✔ SmartMoney.com has a program also called Asset Allocator, which comes up with a formula after a moderately detailed questionnaire.

For details on how to use these programs, ***see*** Part I.

You can readily translate an allocation formula into mutual fund selections at a couple of sites.

Asset allocation at MSN

Follow these steps to figure out how to allocate your assets at MSN Investor:

1. Go to the MSN Investor home page (moneycentral.msn.com/investor).

2. Click Funds.

The Mutual Fund Research page appears.

3. Click Easy Fund Finder.

4. Click Pre-defined Searches.

5. Under the Basic Searches section, click any of the following categories — Small Domestic Stock Fund, Foreign Stock Fund, Large Domestic Stock Fund, or Bond Fund.

Small Domestic and Large Domestic are the same as "small cap" and "large cap." These terms refer to the average market value of the companies owned by the funds, not to the size of the funds themselves.

The figure shows a listing of Small Domestic Stock Funds. MSN ranks funds by one-year total return, although the five-year annualized return figure may be more useful for long-term investors.

6. Click any trading symbol to bring up a fund profile.

Fund profiles list fund fees, availability at online brokers (a useful MSN feature), and links to more detailed information. *See also* "Comparing Costs, Returns, and Risk" in this part for more on this data.

Asset allocation at Fidelity

If you want a true one-stop process for asset allocation and fund selection, try Fidelity's Asset Allocation Planner.

1. Go to the Fidelity site at www400.fidelity.com.

2. Click <u>All Tools</u> and then <u>Asset Allocation Planner</u>.

One caveat: Your allocation will be done only with Fidelity funds. This is a huge family — the biggest of all — but it still covers only a fraction of the available mutual funds.

Asset allocation at Morningstar.com

To search for funds in asset allocation categories at Morningstar.com, the Web site of a much-cited fund rating service, do the following:

1. Go to the Morningstar home page (www.morningstar.com).

2. Click <u>Fund Selector</u>.

3. Click any of the categories in the Pre-set Criteria pull-down menu.

Long-term Winners and Low-Cost U.S.-Stock Funds include (but are not limited to) funds in the domestic large-cap category.

The site displays the search results listed in alphabetical order.

Morningstar rates funds in three ways. One (signified by one to five stars) is a ranking of the funds' risk-adjusted returns within broad groupings. A narrower ranking, also on a one-to-five scale but without the stars, compares funds to peers in narrower categories. A third system compares a fund to its peers based on risk (again on a five-step scale).

4. You can sort your results by performance or some other criteria by clicking the links at the top of each column.

5. To look at the funds' longer-term performance, choose <u>Performance View</u> from the pull-down menu at the top of the table.

If you want to hone in on the large-cap or small-cap categories, go back to the Fund Selector page by clicking Change Criteria. Use the pull-down menu to select from three types of funds: growth, value, and blend.

See also "Choosing Mutual Funds" in this part for more on the "value" and "growth" labels and what they mean.

Buying and Selling Mutual Funds

You have two routes to buying mutual funds:

- ✔ Through brokers
- ✔ Through the funds or fund groups (also called "families") themselves

Trading through brokers

Buying or selling a mutual fund through an online broker is similar to trading a stock. But mutual-fund trades are different in some critical ways:

- ✔ Prices are set just once a day, after the market closes. When you put in an order to buy or sell, you have to accept the *next* available price, which can be the price after the next day's market close if you're buying late in the trading session.

- ✔ In contrast to stock, investors normally buy funds by dollar amount. For instance, you might place an order for $5,000 in shares of no-load Fund XYZ (*no-load* means the fund does not tack on a sales charge). If the broker (not the fund) charges a transaction fee (a commission), you can either take it out of the $5,000 or add it to the total. In a *load* fund, you pay an upfront charge that can be several percentage points of the total purchase price.

- ✔ Stock dividends are usually paid in cash to your brokerage account. Mutual fund shareholders can choose to have dividends (along with capital gains from the fund's sales of stock) re-invested in shares of the fund. In taxable accounts, you have to pay tax on these reinvestments (called "distributions") even if they don't produce any cash.

- ✔ Certain types of trading available for stocks is off-limits for mutual funds. You can't buy funds on margin (though in some cases you can use them as collateral for margin buys of stock), and at most brokerages you can't sell mutual funds short.

To see how a typical online mutual-fund trade works, go to the demo at TD Waterhouse:

1. Go to the TD Waterhouse home page at www.waterhouse.com.

2. Click the Demo tab at the top of the screen.

3. Click <u>Trading</u> on the horizontal menu.

    A stock trading screen appears.

4. Click the Mutual Funds tab.

    A screen for buying funds appears.

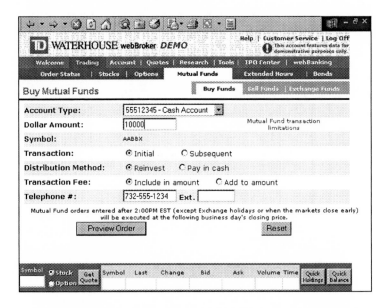

Note the buttons for Initial or Subsequent purchase. This can be an important distinction, because most funds have a higher minimum purchase requirement for first-time buyers than for those who already own shares.

5. Click the Sell Funds tab to see a sell order form.

    From this form, you can either sell by number of shares (not dollar amount) or sell the entire amount.

6. To see an order for exchanging funds — selling shares of one to buy another in one transaction — click the Exchange Funds tab.

Mutual funds, like stocks, are traded online by symbols. All funds have five-letter symbols ending in X. If you don't know a fund's symbol, look it up at the same sites where you would find stock symbols.

- At the Yahoo! Finance home page, use the Symbol Lookup link to the right of the pull-down menu for quotes.

- At MSN Investor, go to Funds and click Find next to the Go button.

Buying and selling direct

If you've discovered a small but brilliantly managed mutual fund that your online broker doesn't carry, you can still invest in it the old-fashioned way — directly with the fund or its family (if it has one).

- You give up some convenience because you can't move your money as readily between this fund and other investments.

- On the other hand, this hurdle may have the benefit of encouraging you to stick with the fund for the long haul.

- Another reason to invest directly with a fund family is the range of the family's own services. Some big ones, like Fidelity and Vanguard, also have online brokerages, where you can buy funds outside the family along with stocks and other investments.

Check a fund's Web site to see if you can apply online (or download a mail-in application) and to see if you can download a prospectus and recent report. *See also* "Downloading prospectuses" for more on this.

One quick route to fund sites is Yahoo! Finance:

1. Go to the home page at finance.yahoo.com.

2. Call up a quote on one or more funds by trading symbol.

3. Click Profile.

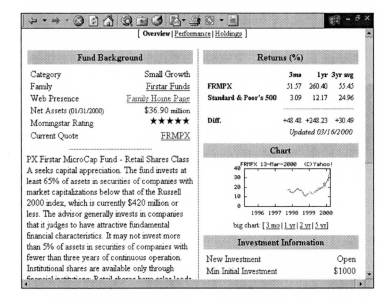

4. In the Fund Background section, check to see what's listed in the Web Presence category. Click Family Home Page if you see that link.

   The Family Home Page link takes you to a Web site with information about investing in the funds and, if available, online applications.

5. If a Web presence isn't listed, scroll down to the Fund Operations section where you should find a phone number to call up the fund and invest the old-fashioned way: by mail.

You might also want to try typing the fund family name in the Web address line of your browser to see what you find. Be sure to add a dot-com domain suffix.

Checking fund family performance

Fund families often have a wide variety of products and make it easy to switch between them. But that convenience may not be worth much if the funds are mediocre. You can compare the performance of fund families as well as individual funds.

To get a quick look at the performance of funds in a few dozen of the largest families:

1. Go to MSN Investor (moneycentral.msn.com/investor).

2. Click Funds and choose a family from the Fund Directory pull-down menu.

You see funds listed with their three-year performance, their objectives, and links to fact sheets.

If you want to reach out to smaller or more obscure families:

1. Go to SmartMoney's mutual fund site (`www.smartmoney.com/intro/funds`).

2. Click <u>Fund Finder</u> in the Fund Tools menu.

3. Click the Family tab.

4. Choose Yes next to Find Funds From A Specific Family.

5. Highlight a fund family that interests you.

6. Click Search.

If the family's not too large, you see all the funds displayed with risk and return data, sales charges, SmartMoney's rankings, and more.

For large families, you have to add criteria using other tabs at the top of the program window to narrow the search.

Downloading prospectuses

You can find out almost all you need to know about a mutual fund from online data and rating services. But you should still look at the fund's own prospectus to see if you might have missed something important. The prospectus details need-to-know items such as marketing and distribution (12b-1) fees, risk factors, and the fund's investment parameters.

✔ If you're buying through a broker, look for a link (or ask for one via e-mail) through which you can order a prospectus. You should always be able to order one to be delivered by mail.

✔ If you aren't working with a broker, some fund families now have downloadable prospectuses and annual reports.

Many prospectuses can be downloaded in PDF format, and many can be viewed online in HTML format as well.

A fund's latest annual report (or semi-annual, if available) is also worth reading for the performance data and list of holdings. Some data may be a bit old by the time you see it, but it does give you a way to test the fund manager's judgment. *See also* "Choosing Mutual Funds."

Choosing Mutual Funds

Mutual funds are often classified within broad categories such as equity (stocks), bond, small-cap, and large-cap. They can also be labeled as "aggressive growth" or "small-cap value." These labels are called *objectives* or *fund types*.

Objectives tell you not only what a fund aims to do, but also what risks it faces. Here are some samples:

- **Aggressive** means high price volatility and, at least in the short term, high risk.

- **Small-cap value** indicates a focus on small companies, usually a volatile area, combined with a bargain-hunting investing style that avoids stocks with high price/earnings ratios.

- **Sector** funds are defined by industry groups, such as telecommunications, biotech, or energy. These tend to be more volatile than the general market.

- **Overseas** funds are divided into several groups, including worldwide, Europe, Japan, and emerging markets. Their risk depends on the size and stability of the market (Western Europe versus developing countries, for instance). For all overseas funds, currency fluctuations add an element of risk not found in domestic funds.

You can use these labels and others to find funds that fit your risk tolerance and preferred asset mix.

Web sites for fund searches usually have several dozen categories, including several for bond funds. *See also* Part IX. In general, most divide stock funds by the average market value ("market cap") of the companies they invest in and whether they focus on "value" (as in "small cap value" above) or growth (which tilts them toward fast-growing companies that may have very high price-earnings ratios).

Searching by objective at Thomson Investors Network

To pick funds by objective, go the Thomson Investors Network (`www.thomsoninvest.net`) and follow these steps:

1. Click the Funds tab.

2. Click <u>Fund Screening</u> under the heading Research.

Doing so takes you to a multi-step search program covering more than 10,000 funds.

3. On the first page of the program, check one or more of the boxes on the list of objectives.

   Clicking just one keeps the list of results manageable.

   Click any link next to a box to see how the objective is defined.

4. Click "Show Results" at the left of the screen to get a list of all funds with your chosen objective.

5. To refine the search further, click one of the links under the Criteria heading.

6. Click the Performance option to screen funds by their return over one or more time frames.

7. Use the pull-down menu to tell the program how critical performance is to you.

8. Click the Show Results button if you want the search to end (although you can also add other criteria, such as expenses and risk).

   A table of funds ranked by their 5-year return appears.

9. Click any trading symbol to call up a chart and fund profile.

Searching by fund type at Morningstar

Most online screens use the categories of the Morningstar rating and research service, or something similar. There are nearly 50 of these categories, covering stocks, bonds, and mixed funds.

To search by fund type at Morningstar, go to the home page at www.morningstar.com and do the following:

1. Click Fund Selector.

2. Choose a fund type from the Fund Type pull-down menu.

3. To narrow a screen based on performance, scroll to Returns and use the pull-down menus to choose returns greater than the category average for one or more periods.

4. Click the Show Results button at the bottom of the page.

   A snapshot view of all the funds in the category that meet your return criteria appears.

5. Choose Portfolio View from the pull-down menu above the chart to get a closer look at the average size of the funds' holdings.

6. Choose Performance View to see the fund's recent and annualized returns, going back as far as 10 years.

   Click the links above any column to rank the listings.

7. Click the name of any fund to call up a profile.

8. Click Portfolio to take a closer look at the fund's holdings and to see how they compare to market averages.

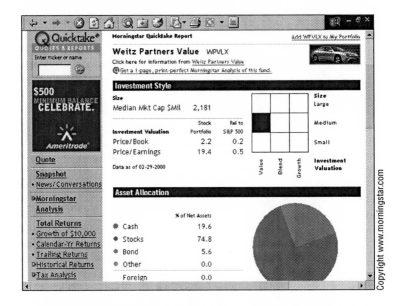

To see how a growth fund differs in style from this, re-run this search using the mid growth category. Or call up funds in the large and small market cap classes to see how their average holdings compare.

TIP

Morningstar lists average figures, for performance and other data, along the top of the fund tables. These are helpful for comparing not only individual funds to their groups but also groups to one another. You can tell whether "growth" or "value" investing is in fashion, for instance, by noting the recent performance averages of fund groups with those labels.

Looking at funds' holdings

If you've done a lot of research into individual stocks, you can put that knowledge to work in analyzing funds. On one of the Morningstar profiles (see the preceding section), click <u>Portfolio</u> and take a look at the top holdings. If you recognize the names and know something about the stocks, you can get a sense of the fund's stock-picking philosophy.

Closed-End Funds

Most mutual funds are *open-end*. That is, they create new shares as new money is invested in them. *Closed-end* funds, a smaller group, have a set number of shares much like a company's stock. In fact, they trade just like stocks.

With open-end funds, investors buy shares directly from the fund (or sell them back) at a price computed daily from the closing values of the fund's securities, minus any debts. This is the net asset value (NAV); it's what fund sellers receive and buyers pay (sometimes with a sales charge, or "load" added on).

With closed-ends, on the other hand, investors buy and sell shares from one another at market prices throughout the trading day.

Since supply and demand set the price, the price you pay or get for shares of a closed-end fund can be a lot different from the NAV. Most closed-ends trade at a discount to NAV — not so good if you buy them at or near the NAV, but possibly a bargain if you're buying them now.

Online data on closed-end funds is skimpy compared to the flood of information on the open-end side. The best site for research is that of the Closed-End Fund Association (CEFA) at www.closed-endfunds.com.

To get a quote, news, and a profile of a particular fund, follow these steps at the CEFA home page:

1. In the Daily NAVs box, type the fund's ticker symbol.

You can also type all or part of its name (such as "Germany" for the New Germany Fund).

2. Click Go.

If you used a ticker symbol, you see a current quote. If you used a keyword, you see a list of matches; click one of these for a quote.

3. From a quote page, click Click Here for More Information on This Fund for a profile.

The profile includes data on the fund's performance, expenses, investment objective, top holdings, and premiums or discounts.

Here are two other useful links on the CEFA page:

✔ Premium and Discount in the Today's Leaders section takes you to lists of the funds trading highest above their NAVs and farthest below them.

✔ <u>Custom Fund Search</u> in the Today's Leaders section enables you to screen closed-end funds by market or NAV return, premium or discount, expense ratio, fund advisor, and type.

Closed-end funds have long been a vehicle for focused investment overseas. Through "country funds," investors can invest in foreign markets with the help of professional management. These markets can still be highly risky, though. For an alternative called "world equity benchmark securities" (WEBS), *see also* "Index Funds."

Comparing Costs, Returns, and Risk

Mutual funds are a relatively cheap way for small investors to benefit from professional money management, but they're not free. Managers (along with sales agents, brokers, and others) all take their share off the top of a fund's market returns. That's one reason why most funds, judged by the actual return to investors, don't consistently beat the market averages.

But some funds do have a record of beating the averages. Some are true bargains — low-cost funds with high returns relative to their risk. Online screens make them easy to find, as the following sections show.

Finding low-cost funds

In judging how much it costs to invest in a mutual fund, you need to look at two kinds of expense: ongoing and one-time:

✔ Ongoing expenses include administration and marketing costs along with the fees paid to the fund's portfolio managers. All funds have ongoing expenses, though these can vary greatly.

✔ One-time costs include sales charges, levied either at the time of purchase (the front-end "load") or when the shares are sold. Many funds don't have either front-end or back-end charges.

For long-term investors, ongoing expenses can make a big difference in return, while one-time charges may fade into insignificance. If you can save 1 percent a year in expenses on a fund investment of $25,000, for instance, your savings adds up to more than $2,500 in 10 years and more than $7,000 in 25.

For ongoing costs, the all-important number is the expense ratio. It's the annual operating costs and management fees of the fund expressed as a percentage of assets. It varies by fund type — it's generally highest for funds that specialize in small, little-known stocks requiring intensive research. But it also varies within fund categories.

Do expense levels matter if a fund is still outperforming its peers? Maybe not in the short term, but high expenses make it that much harder for the portfolio managers to match the performance of more efficient funds over the long run.

To run an expense screen, go to the Morningstar site (www. morningstar.com) and do the following:

1. Click Fund Selector.

2. Pick one fund type from the Morningstar Category pull-down menu.

3. To narrow the search the more efficient funds in the group, choose Category Average from the pull-down menu in the Cost and Purchase section.

   You can also set a maximum initial purchase requirement in a menu just above.

4. To add a performance element to the screen, use the next section of the page to limit funds to those that have beaten their group's average in two or more periods.

5. Click Show Results.

6. Click the Expense Ratio column heading to show the lowest-cost of the group.

7. Click the fund name to call up a profile.

8. Click Nuts and Bolts to get detailed expense data.

   A table with fees, sales charges (if any), and minimum purchase requirements appears.

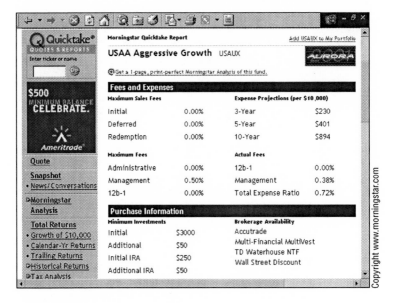

Turnover and tax efficiency

Fund *turnover* is a mark of how active (or hyperactive) a fund's managers have been. Turnover is the volume of shares bought and sold over a year, divided by the total holdings, and expressed as a percentage. A turnover of 100 percent means that a fund traded its whole portfolio (or the equivalent in value) in 12 months.

High turnover isn't necessarily bad, but it can be an issue in taxable accounts.

Funds must distribute their net realized capital gains each year to avoid being taxed on them.

✔ If they've done a lot of buying and selling (in an up year), they're likely to have a lot of realized gains, on which shareholders will owe tax.

✔ A low-turnover fund, on the other hand, will have little realized gains even in a good year, because it sells infrequently. Its shareholders won't have to pay much tax until they sell their own holdings.

Some funds are managed expressly for *tax efficiency* — they buy stocks with little or no dividend yield and keep realized capital gains to a minimum. Other funds (especially index funds) tend to be tax-efficient as a byproduct of their "buy-and-hold" strategy, which shows up in a low turnover rate. They still may pay out substantial taxable dividends.

Tax efficiency is not a concern in IRAs or 401ks because these are simply taxed as ordinary income when the money is withdrawn.

The fund type can also be a clue to its tax consequences.

✔ Funds in an "income" group (or "growth and income") pay dividends that are taxable unless the fund invests in municipal bonds (state and local government debt) that pays tax-exempt interest.

✔ "Balanced" funds (like the "income" group above) are likely to have sizable holdings in taxable bonds.

For a good tutorial on mutual funds and taxes, go to the Vanguard Group site (`www.vanguard.com`), click the Education, Planning & Advice tab, and then click <u>Course 8: Taxes and Mutual Funds</u>.

For tax-free dividends and interest, you can choose from a wide range of funds made up of municipal bonds. Some are limited to bonds issued in one state, making them free from both federal and state taxes for that state's residents. *See also* Part IX. Capital gains from any increase in the value of these funds are taxable, however.

Check carefully before buying a mutual fund for a taxable account toward the end of the year, when dividend and capital-gains distributions are usually paid. If you buy just before a large distribution, you'll pay tax on that amount as if you held the stock all year. And you won't be any richer, since the net asset value of fund shares is always reduced by the amount of the distribution.

See also Part XI.

Risk/return ratios

Risk in investing is simply the danger that the value of your holdings will decrease. Investment types with high returns, such as growth stocks, tend to have commensurately high risk — at least in the near-term. How much of this you can tolerate depends on a lot of things, including your emotional state and how soon you need the money (your time "horizon").

It's best, of course, to have high price appreciation with low risk and low volatility. If you can't have both, then you can at least look for high return relative to the risk.

Here are some methods (and online sites) for gauging a fund's risk/return relationship:

✔ **Bull Market/Bear Market Performance.** Aggressive stock funds can easily look good when stocks in general are rising. But you may not want one that collapses when the market merely sags. To see how a fund did in the most recent major downturn, go to a fund profile at Yahoo! Finance by calling up a quote and clicking <u>Profile</u>. Then click <u>Performance</u> to see how well the fund ran with the bulls and stood up to the bears. You can find this performance data under the Returns Comparison section.

✔ **Alpha.** Alpha tells how much the fund's return exceeds the amount to be expected at its level of risk.

✔ **Beta.** Beta is a fund's volatility in comparison to the overall market (as measured by the Standard & Poor's 500). A beta of 1.00 fluctuates no more or less than the S&P 500.

To read more about the ratios and statistics on a Yahoo! Performance table, click <u>Help</u> at the top of the Yahoo! Finance screen, then click <u>Financial Glossary</u>.

Risk/return screening

You can use beta, alpha, and other ratios at several sites to screen for funds with high return-to-risk profiles. MSN Investor has one of most versatile programs.

1. Go to MSN Investor (moneycentral.msn.com/investor).

2. Click Finder.

3. Click Custom Search in the left-hand menu.

4. Click Funds.

5. In the Finder Wizard dialog box, choose a fund type or choose All for a global search.

6. Click Finish.

7. Click New in the File pull-down menu to start a new search.

8. Click the first blank cell under the heading Field Name for a pull-down menu of screen criteria.

9. Choose the risk/return ratio you want to screen for.

10. Click under the Operator heading for a menu of mathematical operators such as >=, <=, Low as Possible, and so on. Choose one.

11. Click under the Value heading and choose Custom Value. Type a number in the text box.

12. Repeat Steps 8 through 11 to screen for other risk ratios and any other screen criteria you want to use.

13. Click the Run Search button when you're done.

The results appear.

The funds are ranked, with the fund best combining these features on top. Click any trading symbol to learn more about the fund.

Index Funds

If you can't outguess the market, why not buy it? That's the theory behind *index funds*, which seek to imitate the performance of a market average such as the Standard & Poor's 500.

Indexing has a cost advantage over actively managed funds, because its portfolio building process is a no-brainer: The fund simply holds stocks in the same proportion as the index it is following, and you don't need a high-priced stock-picker to do that.

Index funds also tend to have low turnover. Every so often the keepers of an index have to "rebalance" it by dropping some companies and adding others, or buying and selling shares of companies already in it. But only a small fraction of an index fund's shares change hands that way in a given year.

To see a list of top-performing index funds:

1. Go to the Bloomberg site (www.Bloomberg.com).

2. Click <u>Mutual Funds</u> under the Money heading.

3. In the pull-down menu under Look Up Fund by Sector, choose Index.

4. Click Go.

A table of index funds with high short-term performance (ranked by year-to-date returns) appears.

5. To see rankings by long-term performance, choose Long Term Returns under the Change View section and click Go.

6. Click a fund name to call up a brief profile, with a summary of its objective (including the index it follows), a chart, annualized returns for different periods, and a table showing similar funds.

Indexing is not necessarily low-risk investing. Even the broadest market index goes down in a bear market, and some index funds ride some very wild horses, such as technology or Internet indexes and stock-index futures contracts.

Part IX

Bonds

The Internet isn't just for stock pickers. It's also a window into the world of bonds. You can research and buy debt securities of all kinds on the Web — Treasuries, corporates, agencies, municipal bonds — not to mention mutual funds that invest in bonds or a mix of bonds and stocks. If you're a fixed-income investor or wondering if you should be, read on to see the online sites and tools that can help you.

In this part . . .

Bond Investment Strategies

Who should buy bonds? The answer depends on your own circumstances and attitude toward risk. In general, experts advise moving assets into the *fixed-income* category (bonds and similar securities) for the following reasons:

- ✔ When you're nearing retirement and you will want more income from your investments, as well as less volatility.

- ✔ When you need money in the short term.

Here's one allocation formula that has been used by many advisors: Subtract your age from 100, and use that number as the percentage of your portfolio you place in stocks, with the rest in bonds (or liquid investments like money-market funds).

Bonds are less volatile than stocks and provide reliable income. On the other hand, they don't have the growth potential of stocks. The longer you can wait before you need to cash in, the more investing in stocks makes sense for you.

To get some guidance from financial planning tools, **see also** Part I.

SmartMoney has an allocator just for bonds, too. To use it:

1. Go to the SmartMoney home page (`www.smartmoney.com`).

2. Click the Bonds tab.

3. Click <u>Bond Investing</u> in the In Bonds column.

   A page with links to research and education sites appears. You can make choices form either a pull-down menu or a table of contents.

4. Choose Bond Allocation from the pull-down menu, or click that link under What to Buy.

   If you haven't done the general asset allocation I describe in Part I of this book, click <u>SmartMoney One.</u>

   The bond allocator divides your investments between "safe" and "aggressive" depending on your financial needs, risk tolerance, and outlook for the economy.

5. Use your cursor to move the needle along any of the horizontal lines and watch the pie chart change shape.

   Pointing the cursor at any topic brings up an explanation just to the left.

"Safe" and "aggressive" are relative terms in bond investing. Even the safest fixed-income strategy, such as keeping your money in high-grade short-term interest-bearing debt such as Treasury bills, isn't safe from inflation. And longer-term bonds with sterling credit ratings can still suffer in a climate of rising interest rates. In general, though, an "aggressive" bond investor would be looking for either high income (through lower credit-grade "junk" bonds) or capital appreciation by buying long bonds and betting on falling interest rates.

For more on income and profit strategies, with their risks and rewards, click Investing for Income and Investing for Profit on the SmartMoney Bond Investing page.

Bond Funds

If you have enough money on hand, you can build a diversified portfolio of bonds by buying them online in various types and maturities (*see* "Building a bond ladder" later in this part). However, this may not be a practical strategy for an investor who's starting out small. Bonds are usually sold in denominations of $5,000, and dealers sometimes require a minimum investment of $20,000.

With bond mutual funds, you can build your bond portfolio at a lower cost. In return, you have to pay fund costs that cut into your interest income, but you can shop around for funds that keep those expenses to a minimum.

Screening funds

Bond funds cover a wide range of categories, defined both by the type of issuers (corporations, U.S. or foreign governments, states, cities, counties) and by the level of risk.

To see how one well-known research service sorts them out by expense, return, and risk, go to the Morningstar site (www.morningstar.com), and follow these steps:

1. Click Funds and then Fund Selector.

2. Use the pull-down menu next to the heading Morningstar Category in the Fund Type section to pick one of the bond fund categories.

There are about 20 fund types, if you include the "hybrid" funds that invest in a mix of stocks and bonds.

3. To look for the cheapest funds, scroll down to the menu titled Expense Ratio Less Than and choose 0.50%.

4. To narrow the list and weed out the weaker performers, use the pull-down menus under the Returns heading to select funds with 1- 3- and 5-year returns above the category average.

5. To set a limit for risk, go to the heading Average Credit Quality in the Portfolio section and choose A or Higher.

6. Click Show Results.

7. Click <u>Expense Ratio</u> to rank the funds with the cheapest first.

   A results screen appears.

8. To see which funds have good long-term performance, choose Performance View from the pull-down menu.

9. Click the name of any fund to show a profile, including data on its annual returns for the past several years, its risk rating, and purchase information.

The profile of a typical intermediate bond fund is quite different from those in the higher-risk groups, such as High-Yield or Emerging Markets Bond. Try running a screen on the Morningstar program for funds in those two categories.

Watch the Annual Returns table in bond fund profiles. The volatility can be high, especially in emerging-markets funds.

Using ready-made screens

If you know just what kind of fund you're looking for, you can run custom screens with criteria at Morningstar.com. **See also** Part VIII.

If you're not such a do-it-yourselfer, you might try some of these ready-made screens, depending on your investment goals:

✔ If you're looking for capital preservation, try Morningstar's Fund Selector. From the Morningstar home page (www.morningstar.com):

   1. Click Funds and then <u>Fund Selector</u>.

   2. From the Preset Criteria menu, choose Conservative Bond Funds and click <u>Show Results</u>.

      You see a list of funds in several categories (maybe even high-yield) that share a low-risk profile.

✔ For a list of general-purpose bond funds, go to MSN Investor home page (www.moneycentral.msn.com/investor) and then:

1. Click Funds.

2. Click Bond Fund from the Fund Finder pull-down menu.

> You see a list of funds ranked by their 5-year annual returns with expense ratios, one-year returns, and links to profiles (click the trading symbols).

✔ Also at MSN Investor, look at the "pre-defined" searches list for any bond-fund screens.

1. At the home page, click Finder in the horizontal menu. Then click Pre-defined Search and Funds at the left.

2. Look for the High-Yield Bond Fund link to see funds that managed to keep their volatility low in an inherently risky market.

✔ To see the top 25 performers in various bond-fund categories, based on their return over a time-frame of your choice, go to the SmartMoney site (www.smartmoney.com) and then:

1. Click Funds and then click Top 25 Funds under the Fund Tools section.

2. Use the pull-down menus to select a return period (from 13 weeks to 5 years) and a fund category.

3. Click Go.

✔ To see Bloomberg's ranking of funds by total return, go to www.Bloomberg.com and then:

1. Click Mutual Funds in the left-hand column under the Money heading.

2. Click Today's Top Funds under the Mutual Funds heading.

3. Use one pull-down menu over the top funds table to focus on a fund sector, another to view either long-term or short-term returns.

Be careful not to confuse "return" with "yield." *Return* is yield plus (or minus!) change in net asset value. It's the figure to watch in a mutual fund, because it tells you what investors in the fund actually make. *Yield* is the average yield of the bonds in the fund's portfolio. When it's high and the fund's asset value stays steady or rises, that's great. But when the NAV falls (and it can sometimes fall a lot, especially in volatile high-yield funds), you can actually lose money overall.

Closed-end bond funds

Just like stocks, the bond world has closed-end as well as open-end funds. As with closed-end stocks, investors buy shares in these funds in trading on the stock market rather than directly from the funds.

The trading of fund shares sets their price by supply and demand, thereby adding an element of risk or potential reward that is lacking in other bond funds:

✔ If the market turns negative toward a closed-end fund, it can trade at a discount to the underlying value of the bonds it holds (its net asset value, or NAV).

✔ If you buy a fund at a deep discount, you can watch the market rediscover it and then see it trade close to NAV or even at a premium.

Even if the fund stays at a discount, you can still enjoy a boost in yields. When you pay 90 cents on the dollar to buy a batch of bonds yielding 6 percent, you're actual yield is 6.7 percent.

The best source for closed-end fund data (and investor education) is the Closed-End Fund Association site (`www.closed-endfunds .com`). To get a quick look at available bond funds, both taxable and tax-free, click <u>Custom Search</u> under the Today's Leaders heading. Choose one of the bond categories in the Asset Classification window and then click Submit.

See also Part VIII for more on the features of the Closed-End Fund Association's Web site.

Bond Types

Bonds share one thing in common — they're all, in one form or another, a promise to pay back borrowed money, usually with interest. Beyond that, they come in a vast variety, covering a wide range of risks, potential returns, and issuers from all over the world.

For most investors, who don't intend to become bond-trading specialists, these are the main categories to know:

✔ ***Corporate.*** This is debt issued by for-profit businesses. It ranges in credit quality from "gilt-edged" (extremely safe) bonds to the "junk bonds" (those rated as having significant credit risk) that make up portfolios of high-yield mutual funds. The lowest grade is that of bonds issued by companies in default.

✔ **Treasury.** These are debt securities issued directly by the Treasury Department and backed by the United States government. They are the world's benchmark for safe investing, which also puts their yields at the low end of the scale.

Treasuries are labeled by maturity: *Bills* take up to a year to mature; *notes,* up to 10 years; *bonds,* up to 30. Some Treasury issues have yields periodically adjusted for inflation. Longer-term bonds can change significantly in value, for better or worse, with changes in the interest-rate environment.

✔ **Agency.** These are bonds issued by government-sponsored entities rather the Treasury itself. Examples are securities issued by Fannie Mae (Federal National Mortgage Association) and Ginnie Mae (the Government National Mortgage Association).

✔ **Municipal.** These are bonds issued by state or local governments. Their interest is free from federal taxation except when the bonds have a substantial benefit to private parties. Since "munis" are also free from state taxes where they're issued, fund families sell "double tax-free" funds in some of the larger states. The tax exemption of mutual fund interest does not extend to capital gains.

The tax-free status of municipal bonds lowers their yields below that of taxable bonds with the same level of risk. So munis and municipal-bond funds are not appropriate for tax-exempt or tax-deferred accounts such as IRAs.

✔ **Zero-Coupon.** A type of bond (it can be in any of the preceding categories) that does not make regular interest payments at a stated "coupon" rate as other bonds do. Instead of getting payments, holders buy the bond at a discount and get their return from its rising value as it progresses toward maturity. In a taxable "zero," holders pay tax each year on this rising value even though they get no cash. This is not a problem in tax-deferred accounts.

✔ **International.** Bonds issued by foreign governments and businesses cover many types and risk levels. Small investors' best access to them is through mutual funds, including funds with a stock-bond mix.

✔ **Convertible.** Corporate bonds that can be exchanged for another type of security, usually common stock, at a predetermined price. This feature is designed to make them more attractive to investors by adding growth potential. Investors can buy convertibles either directly or through mutual funds that specialize in them. ***See also*** "Bond Funds" in this part.

Buying and Selling Bonds Online

The bond market, long dominated by big institutional traders, has not been as fast as the stock market to offer its products to small investors on the Internet. And online bond traders don't have the huge selection of free data and research that's available to their stock-trading counterparts.

Online mutual-fund marketplaces do have plenty of bond funds, though. For more on these, *see* "Bond Funds" in this part. And more Internet brokers have bond centers where you can trade a wide range of government and corporate issues.

For current information on the best online brokers for bond investing, go to Claire Mencke's Bonds/Fixed Income site at About.com. (www.bonds.about.com/finance/bonds/mbody.htm). Click Bond Investor's Broker Screen in the In the Spotlight section. *See also* "Research and Education" in this part.

Other brokers with good demonstration sites, for education as well as mock online transactions, include:

- ✔ **E*TRADE** (www.etrade.com): Click Bonds in the left-hand column and then click View Bond Center Demo. (Or click Enter Bond Center if you're already a customer.)

- ✔ **DLJdirect** (www.dljdirect.com): Register and log in as a guest user if you need to do so, and then do the following:

    1. Click Trading in the horizontal menu and then click Fixed Income Center in the left-hand menu.

    2. Click Quick Picks for lists of bonds in various categories and maturities.

    3. Click one of the links.

    A screen appears showing a list of bonds issued by corporations and traded on the New York, American, or NASDAQ Stock Markets.

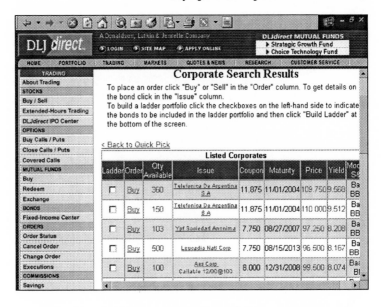

The Coupon and Yield columns both show interest rates, but the latter is what you'll actually get if you buy the bond. The *coupon* is rate annually paid as a percentage of the face value. The *yield* is the interest as a percentage of the actual market price. When the market price is above the face value, the yield is lower than the coupon. When the market price is lower, the yield is higher.

4. To continue to find out about an issue, click one of the links under the Issue column.

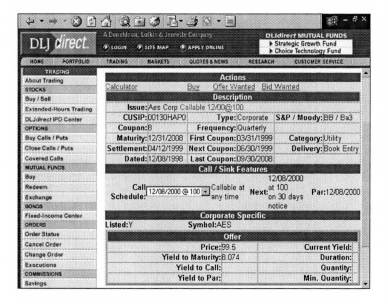

A description appears and gives you basic data about the issue, including price, yield, maturity date, and ratings by Standard & Poor's and Moody's.

5. To buy any bond (be sure to thoroughly investigate any bond before purchasing it), click the <u>Buy</u> link under the Order heading.

   Remember: You can only purchase the number available in the Quantity column.

   A screen appears giving you three options for buying a bond: at the *market* (similar to a market order for stock shares) or at a specified *price* or *yield.*

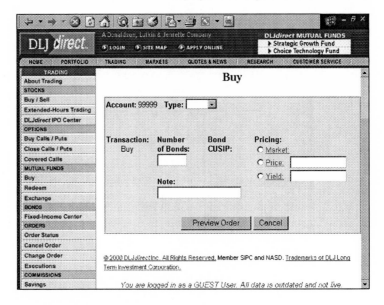

6. Click any of the purchasing links to see a definition.

   See also "Price Data" in this part.

 When you purchase a bond, you're asked for the CUSIP number. *CUSIP* (short for Committee on Uniform Securities Identification Procedures) is a numbering system for all bonds and stocks registered for public trading. It enables a broker or an online trading system to look up exactly the bond issue you're buying. At E*TRADE, you can find the CUSIP numbers in the detailed issue data, reached through the links described previously in Step 4.

Building a bond ladder

You can use an online trading site to buy a *ladder* of bonds with different maturity dates. Building a bond ladder is a way to balance your portfolio between longer-term bonds, which tend to have higher yields but are more volatile in price, and shorter term bonds that pay slightly less but will be redeemed sooner.

For a demonstration of how to build a bond ladder, go to the DLJdirect site (www.dljdirect.com) and then do the following:

1. Click Trading and then click Fixed Income Center.

2. Click Ladder Demo under the Resources and Education heading.

   A table of bonds listed by years to maturity appears.

 3. Check off boxes in the left-hand side to include bonds in your ladder.

 4. Click <u>Build Ladder </u>to see tables showing the different maturities and yields along with the annual and monthly income you'll receive.

You can go through a similar laddering demonstration at E*TRADE by going to the Bond Center page. Go to the home page (www.etrade.com), click <u>Bonds </u>and then click <u>Enter Bond Trading Demo</u>.

Trading costs

Transaction costs for bond buyers and sellers come in two forms:

 ✔ The broker's transaction fee

 ✔ The spread — the difference between what buyers pay and sellers receive.

On large orders, you may not pay a fee, but the broker — acting as a principal — can still make money on the spread.

You can get E*TRADE's current fee list by going to the Bond Center:

 1. Go the home page (www.etrade.com).

 2. Click <u>Bonds</u> and then click <u>Enter Bond Trading Demo</u>.

 3. Click <u>Transaction Fee Schedule.</u>

 For other questions you may have on bond trading, visit the <u>Read our FAQs</u> link.

 4. To see how much the bid-offer spread can cost you and how it varies with the size of an order, return to the Bond Center page and click <u>Quick Picks</u>.

 5. Click one of the links under the headings Treasuries, Treasury STRIPS, or Live Municipals.

 A results screen lists bonds with two prices and yields. The higher price (with the lower yield) is the offer or asking price — what sellers will accept. The lower price (and higher yield) is the bid, or what buyers are willing to pay.

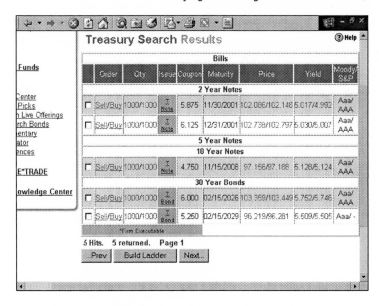

6. To see how volume discounts can narrow a bid/offer spread, click an issue name.

   A screen of data appears, showing how the offer (asking) price changes with order size.

   Quoted bond prices are based on a par value of $100, but the bonds themselves are issued in increments of $1,000. So you need to multiply the quoted price by 10 to find out the minimum you would have to pay. If you want to buy a Treasury bond priced at $97.28, you'll pay $972.80 (plus any transaction fee) per bond.

Buying through TreasuryDirect

You can buy U.S. Treasury issues — bonds, notes, and bills — either through a broker or directly from the government at one of its regular auctions.

To bypass brokers (and transaction fees) and buy directly online from the government through its TreasuryDirect program:

1. Go to the home page of the Bureau of the Public Debt (www.publicdebt.treas.gov).

2. Click TreasuryDirect Electronic Services.

   A virtual lobby appears.

3. If you have an account, you can click Continue to access it.

4. If you don't have an account, click the <u>TreasuryDirect</u> link.

5. To read an overview of how the program works, click <u>Fre-</u>
   <u>quently Asked Questions (FAQ)</u> and then read the
   TreasuryDirect section.

6. Hit the Back button to return to the main TreasuryDirect page.

7. Click Opening an Investor Account.

   This opens a page that briefly explains accounts and account
   services.

8. Click <u>PDF 5182, "New Account Request"</u>.

9. Check the table of available forms to find PDF 5182.

   Use a pull-down menu to specify a quantity (one or two) and
   then click the download icon if you see one. If the download
   option isn't available, you can order forms to be mailed to you —
   see the <u>Enter Mailing Address </u>link.

10. Click the download icon to download a PDF and PostScript file.

    After you fill out and mail in your application, you can dis-
    pense with paper. Buy Treasury securities and maintain your
    account online through the virtual lobby.

You may not associate staid old U.S. Savings Bonds with Internet
investing, but the Bureau of the Public Debt does offer these bonds
online. You can even pay for them with your Visa or MasterCard.

1. At the Bureau's home page (`www.publicdebt.treas.gov`),
   click <u>Savings Bonds</u>.

2. Click <u>Savings Bond Connection</u>.

3. If you're ready to buy, click <u>Go Shopping</u> and follow the
   instructions.

Price Data

Online bond data, especially what you can get for free, doesn't
match the size and scope of all the readily available information
about stocks. But you can use the Internet without much trouble to
follow trends in bond prices and get the standard ratings on bond
quality.

One bond number — the current yield on the 30-year Treasury
bond — is almost as widely reported as the Dow Jones Industrial
Average. It's called the *bellwether bond* because it's used by financial markets to gauge the interest-rate climate in general, just as
the Dow 30 gauges the health of the entire stock market.

Bond quotes at CNNfn

At a number of Web sites, you can also follow other key interest rates, such as shorter-term treasuries, munis, and corporates. CNNfn is especially good for this. From its home page (`www.cnnfn.com`):

1. Click Bonds & Rates under Markets.

2. Click Latest Rates for a summary of Treasuries, municipal bonds, and corporate bonds in short to long maturities.

3. Click <u>Municipal</u>, <u>CMO</u>, or <u>Zero-Coupon</u> for more focused searches on those categories. (a CMO — collateralized mortgage obligation — is a type of mortgage-backed bond).

4. Click Find Bonds to get the results.

5. You can get details on each of these bonds by clicking the links in the Issue column.

Bond quotes at CBS MarketWatch

Another good site for bond quotes is CBS MarketWatch. At the home page (`www.cbs.marketwatch.com`), click <u>Market Data</u> in the main menu. Then click any of the links under the Bonds heading in the table of contents. Click <u>Corporates</u> to call up a Bellwether Bonds Report.

Report tables give corporate bond prices in three lower grades. For each bond, the table lists data including the coupon, maturity date, the economic sector of the issuing company, the value, the change up or down, and the yield to maturity or yield to call (***see also*** the Glossary).

Ratings

The yield and price of a bond are intimately tied to its credit rating, and two firms dominate the rating field: Moody's Investors Service and Standard & Poor's. You'll see their ratings cited both for individual bonds and in classifying mutual funds.

In shopping for both bonds and funds, understanding what the ratings mean is important:

✔ Ratings do not cover all risks. Even a triple-A rated bond isn't immune from *market risk*, in which rising interest rates may force the bond's yield to go higher and its price to lower.

✔ Ratings deal only with the ability of a company (or government or non-profit agency) to pay its debts.

Here's how to go online at the Moody's and Standard & Poor's sites to get a full explanation of the rating codes:

✔ **Moody's** (www.moodys.com): From the home page, click <u>Ratings & Rating Actions</u>. At the top of the next page, click <u>How to Use Ratings</u> for an overview and then click <u>Rating Definitions</u> for detailed explanations of ratings on various types of debt, short-term and long.

✔ **Standard & Poor's** (www.standardandpoors.com): At the company home page, click <u>Ratings Services Home</u>. Click <u>Corporate Ratings</u> and then click <u>Ratings Definitions</u>. Bond ratings are explained under <u>Issue Credit Ratings.</u>

Click <u>Rating Outlook Definitions</u> in the Issue Credit Ratings section for an explanation of Standard & Poor's CreditWatch, in which a company is placed under special scrutiny because of potential credit problems. Such an event can have an impact on a company's stock as well as its bond prices.

Research and Education

Several sites are good starting points for the investor who wants to follow the bond market and learn more about bond investing:

✔ **Investing in Bonds** (www.investinginbonds.com): This is the education site of the Bond Market Association, the trade group for securities firms and banks that underwrite, trade, and sell bonds and other debt securities. Go to the home page and click the links under the Getting Started heading if you're new to bonds. Or click <u>Read It Now!</u> under the Bond Basics heading.

Look under the Free Bond Price Info heading for links to daily municipal and corporate bond prices (*see also* "Price Data" in this part). Under the Investor's Guides heading are links to tutorial sites on different bond types such as municipal bonds, zero-coupon bonds, corporate bonds, and mortgage securities.

✔ **Bonds/Fixed Income at About.com** (www.bonds.about.com/finance/bonds/mbody.htm): Bond expert Claire Mencke, co-author of *Teach Yourself Investing Online* (published by IDG Books Worldwide, Inc.), runs this site. Go to the home page and browse the links in the Subjects menu for data resources, news, bond brokers, and more. The In the Spotlight section has links to useful articles on subjects such as bond public offerings, bonds and taxes, and bond-market trends.

Part X

Tracking Investments

The Internet is ideal for making lists of stocks and other investments and then following their performance. You want to track two kinds of portfolios — those with securities you already own, and *watch lists* of stocks you're just considering. This part shows you how to keep these lists and, with the help of desktop software, measure portfolio performance.

In this part . . .

Creating Watch Lists

Keeping one or more *watch lists* of stocks you don't own serves at least two purposes:

✔ First, watch lists help you figure out when and if a stock is a good buy. They can give you a heads-up when a stock reaches a desirable price or shows a price-volume pattern that signals a good buy.

✔ Second, watch lists help you learn the fundamentals of a stock better. By watching news and financial reports as they come out, you get to know a lot about a company and its products, its prospects, and what analysts are saying about it.

In general, setting up an online watch list is just a simpler version of creating a portfolio. You enter stock symbols and (depending on the Web site's features) price targets and indexes.

Numerous financial Web sites have investment monitoring tools. Usually, you have to register (for free) at the site to customize it for watch lists and portfolio tracking.

 News alerts, offered either through your broker or through financial portal sites, are another way of learning about buy (and sell) points. *See also* Part VI for information on setting up news alerts.

Watch lists at Yahoo! Finance

Yahoo! Finance is a good place to call up multiple quotes quickly, making it ideal for watching lists. Lists are easy to set up (after you register) and edit. The lists benefit from the wide range of optional data that Yahoo! lets you use to customize quotes.

To build a stock-tracking list with a focus on price and volume (the better to spot buy signals), do the following:

1. Go to the Yahoo! Finance home page (www.quote.yahoo.com or www.finance.yahoo.com).

2. If you already registered, click <u>Create</u> in the line of links next to the Portfolios heading.

If you haven't registered, click <u>Customize</u> and then follow the instructions for new users.

3. Under My Portfolios, click Create New Portfolio.

4. In the upper part of the portfolio editing screen, fill in boxes with the portfolio name (try "Watch List") and symbols of the stocks you want to follow.

5. Scrolling down, choose any market indexes you want to include, and state your preferences for how the list is to be displayed.

Yahoo! asks you whether you want the total value of the portfolio displayed. Because you're creating a watch list, you'd probably say no. This is a useful feature, though, for lists of stocks and securities you own.

6. Further down the bottom of the page, use the pull-down menu after Default View for This Portfolio to select the quote style you want. *See also* Part II.

You can edit any of these default styles. *See also* "Editing your portfolio display" in this part.

7. Under the Step 4: Advanced Features heading, skip the first four boxes, which apply only to stocks or funds you already own.

To set up price-limit reminders, click the Upper Limit and Lower Limit checkboxes.

8. Click the Enter More Info button.

9. In the next screen to appear, fill in the price limit boxes next to the symbols to set up alerts on Yahoo! Messenger.

You can get a reminder when a stock rises above an upper limit or falls below a lower limit. *See also* Part VI for more on setting up alerts.

10. Click the Finished button.

The quotes for your watch-list stocks appear.

To refresh the quotes, just click the link bearing the name of your list to the right of the Portfolios heading. To edit the list (add or delete stocks, change preferences, and so on), click the Edit link just after the list name. To change the data mix, click Edit after the name of the quote type (such as DayWatch, Basic, and so on). For more on these options, *see also* "Editing your portfolio display" in this part.

Watch lists at Quicken.com

The Quicken.com Web site truly shows its potential when you use it to track and analyze an actual portfolio (especially if you have Quicken home-finance software). But it's still a good place to set up a watch list. Quicken.com enables you to program a wide range of alert triggers in price and volume action for your watch-list stocks.

See also Part VI for more on setting up alerts.

To create a watch list:

1. Go to the Quicken.com Investing home page (`www.quicken.com/investments`) and click the Investing tab.

2. Click <u>Portfolio</u>.

3. Click Create New Portfolio.

   A dialog box appears asking you to choose whether to create a standard portfolio or an investment account with data imported from your brokerage.

   Both Quicken.com and MSN Investor can import data from brokerage accounts, though only a few online brokers currently participate. For other types of data import and export, *see also* "Transferring Data to and from the Web" in this part.

4. Click Create a Standard Portfolio.

5. For creating a watch list, enter the symbols in the left-hand column and leave the Optional Data section of the grid blank.

6. Scroll down the page and choose indexes to include in your watch list and a few customizations in your data display.

7. Click Finished.

   Your watch list is displayed as the table of quotes.

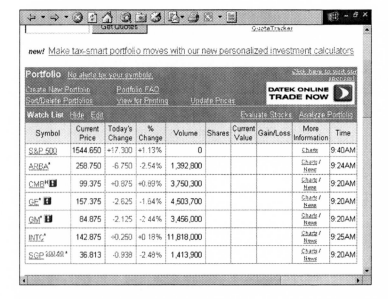

Symbol	Current Price	Today's Change	% Change	Volume	Shares	Current Value	Gain/Loss	More Information	Time
S&P 500	1544.650	+17.300	+1.13%	0				Charts	9:40AM
AREA*	258.750	-6.750	-2.54%	1,392,800				Charts / News	9:24AM
CMB**	99.375	+0.875	+0.89%	3,750,300				Charts / News	9:20AM
GE*	157.375	-2.625	-1.64%	4,503,700				Charts / News	9:20AM
GM*	84.875	-2.125	-2.44%	3,456,000				Charts / News	9:20AM
INTC*	142.875	+0.250	+0.18%	11,818,000				Charts / News	9:25AM
SGP 100.60*	36.813	-0.938	-2.48%	1,413,900				Charts / News	9:20AM

Exclamation marks and other icons next to some trading symbols signal alerts. Click them for details.

Watch lists at MSN Investor

Microsoft's MSN Investor site enables you to quickly set up watch lists along with more exhaustive portfolio tracking and analysis tools. Watch for the FYI links in the portfoliodisplay — these signal news stories, price moves, and other significant events.

Here's how to create a simple MSN watch list:

1. At the MSN Investor home page (`www.moneycentral.msn .com/investor`), click Portfolio on the main menu bar.

If you're registered and have all the software you need, go to the File menu on the Portfolio screen and click New Account. This calls up the Portfolio Manager New Account Wizard box.

If you haven't registered as an MSN Passport user, you can do so now. Just follow the on-screen instructions. You may also have to download software at this point to make the portfolio program work.

2. Choose Watch under the Account Types heading and click Next.

An Enter Watch Account Information box appears.

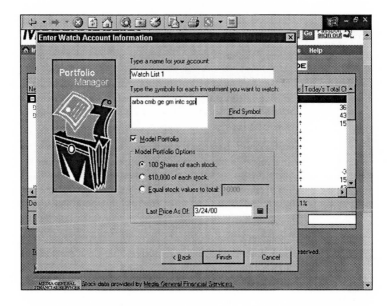

3. Type an account name and list of trading symbols.

4. Click Finish to display a list with current quotes.

MSN enables you to set up a watch list with something extra — mock portfolio pricing. In the Enter Watch Account Information box, you can set up such a list by checking the Model Portfolio checkbox and choosing one of three options to measure performance.

Online Portfolio Analysis

After you plug in your stock and fund symbols along with the benchmark purchase data, you can start getting answers to the big questions: Are your investments following your plan? Are they measuring up to your goals?

The simplest question is probably "what are we worth today?" — what is the bottom-line, current value of all your holdings?

✔ **AOL** (at the Personal Finance channel): Current value is shown in the portfolio display, along with the dollar-value and percentage change for that day.

✔ **Quicken.com Investing** (www.quicken.com/investments): Call up your portfolio display by clicking Portfolio (*see also* "Recording buys and sells"). From the Show Me pull-down menu, choose Portfolio Value. The bottom line of your portfolio table will show the latest total portfolio value, the change on the day and the change since the portfolio started.

✔ **Yahoo! Finance** (www.finance.yahoo.com): Click a portfolio link (listed after Portfolios). Your portfolio display shows the total value, change for the day, cumulative value, and overall change at the bottom of the table. Annualized gains and losses are shown for individual securities but not for the portfolio as a whole.

If you don't see these totals, you may have inadvertently turned off this feature. Click Edit alongside the portfolio name and then go to Step 3: Basic Features. Make sure the Don't Show the Portfolio Total Value on your My Yahoo! Pages box is not checked. Click the Finished button at the bottom of the page.

✔ **MSN Investor** (www.moneycentral.msn.com/investor): Click Portfolio at the home page. The total market value of the portfolio is shown just below the chart, along with the daily and cumulative changes. At the bottom of the page are portfolio totals. To select accounts for totaling (and to delete a "mock portfolio" watch list that would distort your totals), use the pull-down Accounts menu at the top of the portfolio display.

You can show the listed accounts one at a time, or show any combination of them by clicking Select Accounts.

Portfolio analysis at MSN Investor

The MSN Investor portfolio display can take you to a quick analysis of your portfolio performance and asset allocation. At the MSN Investor home page (`www.moneycentral.msn.com/investor`), follow these steps:

1. Click Portfolio to call up a display of your investments.

2. From the Analysis pull-down menu, click Portfolio Charting to get snapshots of asset allocation and performance.

3. From the Chart pull-down menu on the Portfolio Charting window, choose either Investment Performance, Investment Allocation, or Investment Value.

   If you choose Investment Performance, use the Period pull-down menu to pick a time-frame.

   To choose a comparative index (such as the NASDAQ Composite), use the Options menu. Choosing Type from the Chart By section produces a simple bar chart comparing how your individual stocks and mutual funds have done.

4. Close the window to return to the portfolio display.

5. Go to the Analysis menu again and click Portfolio Review.

   MSN gives you charts and tables covering both asset and risk analysis of your holdings.

   The top of the screen shows how your portfolio is divided among asset classes and among capitalization categories of stock.

   Further down, you can see your risk profile — how your holdings are split between low, medium, and high-risk investments.

   This overview includes not only stocks and other securities you own individually, but holdings of your mutual funds as well.

6. Again, close the window to return to the portfolio display.

Portfolio analysis at Quicken.com

To get a more detailed look at your portfolio's asset allocation from Quicken.com, go to the Investing home page (`www.quicken.com/investments`) and click Portfolio. When the display appears:

1. Click Asset Allocation.

2. Check off which portfolio you want to analyze, and then click Go.

3. You then see a chart showing your portfolio allocation, with several links alongside it. Choose <u>Model Allocation</u>, <u>Security Diversification</u>, or <u>Sector Diversification</u>, to see graphs, charts, and discussions about the balance (or lack thereof) in your holdings.

Tracking Your Portfolio Online

Tracking your investments can be quite a burden if you have several accounts (at a broker, a mutual fund, and a 401(k), for instance). Even if you religiously file all the trade confirmations and carefully read your regular account statements, you still may have only a vague idea of how your overall portfolio is doing.

Your broker's online account statements and transaction histories help some. And recording investments with desktop financial software such as Quicken or Microsoft Money can help a lot, as this section shows.

However, an Internet-based portfolio is hard to beat if you want a comprehensive, one-page view of all your investments with prices updated automatically.

Such an overview gives you a way of spotting your winners and losers as well as keeping track of your bottom line. It helps you spot mutual funds or stocks that are under-performing the market (though it's still up to you to decide whether you'll give them more of a chance or you'll move your money elsewhere).

 If you're following an investing discipline that requires you to sell stocks that drop a certain percentage from their purchase price, you can use portfolio tools to tell you not just when stocks have passed this level, but when they're approaching it.

Portfolio tracking and asset allocation

Portfolio tracking plays an important part in asset allocation. You can use portfolio analysis tools such as those at MSN Investor and Quicken.com to see if your mix of stocks, bonds, and cash, or small-cap to large-cap stocks, fits the mix that you've judge to be right for your situation and goals. *See also* Part I.

You can also see if you're staying well-diversified. Sometimes, individual stocks can soar so fast that they take up too large a part of your overall portfolio, especially if they're high-risk, volatile issues. A portfolio display that shows the percentage share of each holding (as at MSN Investor) can alert you to this type of problem.

First-time portfolio setup

To get the most out of online portfolio tools, you need to set benchmark data for each of your stocks, funds, or other securities. Setting a benchmark gives the program a starting point for measuring your portfolio's performance.

Different programs have different looks, but they all ask for the same information. Plan to enter the purchase date, the number of shares, the purchase price per share, and any commissions into online forms.

Here is how America Online subscribers record transactions in AOL's portfolio tracker:

1. At the Welcome page, click AOL Channels.

2. Click Personal Finance.

3. Click My Portfolios.

4. Click Create to set up a new portfolio.

5. In the first screen of AOL Portfolio Setup, type a name for your portfolio and click the Next button.

6. In the spaces provided, enter symbols and trade data for all the securities you own in this account (or all your accounts, if you're setting up a comprehensive portfolio).

   If you've bought a stock or fund more than once (200 shares a year ago or 100 shares last month, for instance), you need to record each purchase as a separate transaction to get accurate performance data.

   Depending on the program you're using (read its FAQs or Help files to be sure), you may also have to enter stock splits as new sales. Ditto for reinvestments of dividends or capital gains into new shares (as with mutual funds or dividend-reinvestment plans).

7. Click the Next button when you finish entering securities.

8. In the next screen, you have the option of entering your cash balance — the dollar amount you have in money market funds, brokerage cash accounts, and other liquid assets.

AOL lets you track money-market funds by their trading symbols (which you can get from a transaction history at your brokerage). But it's also easy to revise the cash balance manually every month from your account statements.

9. Click the Finish button to display the portfolio.

If the idea of tracking down actual purchase prices and dates for all your stocks and funds is just too daunting, try this shortcut: Pick a date (it can be today) and make that the starting point for measuring your portfolio's performance. Then just plug in the day's closing stock prices and net asset values of mutual funds as purchase prices. Future transactions, along with stock splits and reinvestments of mutual fund distributions, should be recorded as they happen.

For most portfolio programs, follow the preliminary steps for setting up a watch list (*see also* "Creating Watch Lists" in this part), but this time add purchase data and choose Regular account rather than Watch account.

Recording buys and sells

After you set up a portfolio, you need to record any buying or selling action. For buys:

- ✔ **AOL** (at the Personal Finance channel): Record future buys by first calling up the portfolio (click <u>My Portfolios</u>, highlight a portfolio name, and click Display) and then clicking <u>Add</u>.

- ✔ **Yahoo! Finance** (www.finance.yahoo.com): Call up the portfolio by clicking its name on the home page. Click the <u>Edit</u> link next to the portfolio name. Add a stock or fund by typing a new symbol in the Ticker Symbols box and scroll down to the Advanced Features table to type purchase data.

- ✔ **Quicken.com Investing** (www.quicken.com/investments): Display portfolios by clicking <u>My Portfolio</u> at the home page. To add a security, click the <u>Portfolio</u> link after Edit, and then click Add Shares.

- ✔ **MSN Investor** (www.moneycentral.msn.com): Display your portfolio by clicking <u>Portfolio</u> in the horizontal menu at the home page. Then click the Edit pull-down menu at the top of the portfolio display and choose Record a Buy.

As for sales, at most sites you record these by deleting the stock or fund from the portfolio.

✔ **AOL:** You highlight a security on the portfolio display and click Delete.

✔ **Quicken.com and Yahoo! Finance:** You delete trading symbols from the same box that you used to add them to your portfolio.

✔ **MSN Investor:** From the Edit pull-down menu, click Record a Sell. A special menu appears.

If you're selling part of your holdings, reduce the number of shares (in the same area where you first recorded them) but keep the security listed.

Remember: You need to add any proceeds from sales to your cash balance, just as you need to take out the cost of a purchase from cash. MSN Investor portfolios do this automatically when you record a sell.

What about bonds? They're mostly off the radar of online portfolio tracking. You can use data from your broker or a newspaper to manually update a bond's value (which, unlike that of money-market funds, does fluctuate). But at the time of this book's writing, the data feeds used for automatic online portfolio updates don't include prices of individual bonds, though they do follow indexes. Bond mutual funds, however, are tracked by price and trading symbol just as stock funds are.

Editing your portfolio display

Portfolio programs give you various options for data display. In general, you'll probably want to choose the items that help you track performance rather than alert you to buy signals, as a watch list might do.

Yahoo! Finance has a ready-made format for tracking performance on its quote menu. Without further editing, it gives you the value of each holding, its change on the day, and its change since you bought it (with the annualized percentage gain or loss).

To refine the display:

1. With your portfolio displayed on the screen, click the <u>Edit</u> link just to the right of the Performance heading.

2. The Edit Your View screen appears with the menu shown here.

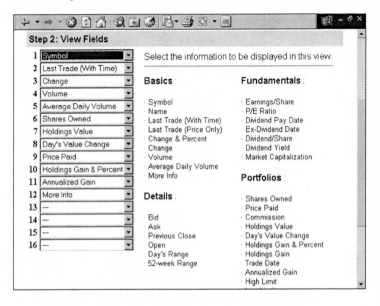

The available data points are listed in several categories on the right; those under the Portfolios heading are of particular interest. The menu on the left has a maximum of 16 spaces, each with a pull-down menu listing all the options.

3. Choose any option for any of the 16 spaces.

   Bear in mind that, unless you have a very wide, high-resolution screen, you have to do a lot of sideways scrolling to see all 16 columns.

4. When you finish updating the display, click Accept Changes at the bottom of the page.

MSN Investor, not to be outdone, has some 70 types of data to choose from in its portfolio display. You can customize your columns or choose from several ready-made views, such as Asset Allocation, Performance, and Valuation.

The asset allocation column is one of the most valuable, because it immediately tells you how large a share each holding takes up in your portfolio. To see the menu of all the data you can add to your portfolio, click Columns just above the portfolio display. You can choose several ready-made data mixes or create your own by choosing Customize Column Set.

Tracking Your Portfolio with Desktop Software

Home finance software such as Quicken and Microsoft Money does more than cut checks and track family budgets. These programs are also good for investment tracking.

The longer you keep records, the more of your investment history you can analyze. If you've been recording your buys, sells, reinvested dividends, and other transactions for several years, you can see how well you've done as an investor over both the near and long-term. You can "report" your own performance as if you were running your own mutual fund. Then you can ask yourself, would anyone invest their money with *you?*

Recording transactions

The cardinal rule of Quicken, Microsoft Money, and other home-finance software is, "Don't Fall Behind." Record transactions in your investment accounts (as well as in your checking account) soon after they occur or show up on your account statements.

This includes reinvestment of dividends and capital gains. Faithfully recording these events can save you a lot of trouble at tax time, as well as help you keep your portfolio value up to date. Always make separate entries for the long-term gains, short-term gains, and dividends reported in your account statement. Each has different impacts on your taxes. *See also* Part XI for more on taxes.

In a reinvestment, a mutual fund distribution or stock dividend is paid in dollars and is used to buy shares (and fractions of shares) based on the security's current price. Often, because of rounding off, the dollar amount divided by the stated number of shares on the account statement does not exactly equal the per-share price. In that case, Quicken recommends adjusting the price.

When you record a buy, the cost is taken out of your cash account. What actually happens, in a typical brokerage account, is that some of your shares in a money market fund are sold to cover the purchase. With a sale of a security, the reverse happens. The proceeds go into buying money-market shares. These produce income for you, and you can record it two ways:

- Record the purchase of the money-market fund shares as a "buy," leaving cash at zero.

  Recording the purchase in this way allows you to track the performance (that is, the dividend income) of your money fund as a separate security.

✔ Leave the cash balance unlabeled (except as "cash") and record interest or dividend payments as they occur, adding them to your balance. This way, you lose some performance data but gain simplicity. *See also* "Exporting Quicken portfolios from desktop to Web" in this part.

Measuring performance with desktop programs

The reward of keeping good records comes when you want to take stock of your investments and, most of all, when you have to pay taxes. *See also* Part XI for more on taxes.

You can take a snapshot of your portfolio performance over any time period, for as far back as you've been keeping track of buys, sells, splits, dividends, and interest.

With Quicken desktop software, take these steps:

1. At the opening page, choose Investing⇨ Investment Performance Report from the Reports pull-down menu.

The default report gives you a year-to-date overview, including the beginning and ending market value, any transfers into and out of the account, and your annualized total return. The latter is the key performance number, because it shows how your investments have performed after correcting for fund transfers.

2. Change this report in a number of ways:

- Use the Customize command at the left to add or take away securities and accounts.

- Use the pull-down menu at the left to choose another time period, or create a custom a time period using the From and To pull-down calendars.

3. Click Update to produce a new report.

An updated report appears.

For further detail, you can subtotal reports by quarters, months, securities, and other criteria. Use the pull-down menu farthest to the right.

To call up investment reports at Microsoft Money:

1. Click Reports at the opening page and then click Investments in the left-hand menu.

You see a number of report options.

The Performance by Investment Account option shows the gains, realized and unrealized, of your securities.

2. Click Customize at the base of this table to change the date range and other settings.

Transferring Data to and from the Web

The Internet is a two-way street for your investment data:

✔ In one direction, there's the download feature of home finance software that updates the prices of stocks and funds in your Quicken or Microsoft Money accounts.

✔ In the other direction, you can upload your portfolio from your desktop to the Web at either Quicken.com or MSN Investor. Some online brokers also allow you to transfer account data from their site to a financial portal.

For any online updates from Quicken or Money, you must first set up an Internet connection according to the software's instructions.

Here are some examples using Quicken 2000 and Money 2000 (earlier versions have similar steps):

Updating prices in Quicken

To update prices in Quicken:

1. Open Quicken and choose Portfolio View from the Investing pull-down menu.

2. From the Update menu, choose Get Online Quotes and follow the instructions from there.

   Note: Securities without trading symbols will not be recorded. *See also* "Recording transactions."

Updating prices in Microsoft Money

To update prices in Microsoft Money:

1. At the opening page, click Investing and then click Portfolio.

2. Under the Common Tasks heading in the left-hand column, click Update Prices for a pull-out menu.

3. Choose Update Price Online.

   If you first want to select certain securities for updating, choose Pick Quotes to Download from the same menu.

Exporting Quicken portfolios from desktop to Web

To export Quicken portfolios from desktop to Web:

1. Open Quicken and choose Investing⇨Portfolio View.

2. Click Portfolio Export and follow the instructions.

> If you're registered at Quicken.com, you can then see your Quicken data at the Web site by going to the Investing home page (www.quicken.com/investments) and clicking Portfolio. This works best if you record money-market fund and interest-bearing accounts simply as "cash" in your Quicken register. Otherwise, you have to add these amounts manually online.

Importing MSN portfolios to Money

To import MSN portfolios to Money:

1. Click Investing on Money's opening page.

2. Under MoneyCentral Synchronization, click the link <u>Synchronize My Money Data with MoneyCentral Now</u>.

Doing so takes you online to MSN Investor, giving you access to quotes and news. If your MSN portfolios includes watch lists, they will be downloaded into Money, also.

Importing portfolios to MSN from Money

To import portfolios to MSN from Money:

1. At the MSN Investor home page (www.moneycentral. msn.com/investor), click <u>Portfolio</u>.

2. Click Import in the File pull-down menu in the portfolio display.

A box asks for the existing account location.

3. Choose On My Computer in Microsoft Money.

4. Click Next and choose either the Import or Link option.

- The Import option brings data from Money to MSN. Later updates you make in the desktop program do not automatically show up in your online portfolio.

- The Link option synchronizes data so that your editing of data in the Money desktop program shows up on your MSN online portfolio. With this option, data can be edited only in the desktop program.

5. Click Next to carry out the transfer.

Tax Consequences of Investing

The price of success can be steep at tax time, especially for investors in high tax brackets, paying state as well as federal income tax and making most of their money in short-term trading. But a careful investor can use the tax code to his advantage and lessen the bite significantly, even in a fully taxable account. The following section sets forth some of the key points of tax-wise investing and shows you where you can find more detailed, current information on the Web.

In this part . . .

Computing Capital Gains

Tax law favors the buy-and-hold investor, especially one who is content to do without dividends. Under the federal statutes currently in effect, gains on the sale of assets held more than one year are taxed at a significantly lower rate than those held for less time.

- ✔ For taxpayers in the 15 percent bracket, the long-term capital gains rate is 10 percent.

- ✔ For those in the 28 percent bracket or higher, it's 20 percent.

- ✔ If you're in the highest bracket, 39.6 percent, you can cut your tax almost in half by holding on to that stock just past the one-year mark.

Differences like these put a premium on good record-keeping. And with desktop software, keeping track of your gains and losses is easy, as long as you update your records faithfully and often.

Tax-preparation software such as TurboTax also makes the job of computing your capital gains taxes much easier than it used to be — as long as you have the transaction data on your computer, ready to crunch.

Capital gains rules don't apply to tax-deferred accounts such as IRAs. The money in these is simply taxed as regular income when you finally withdraw it. But you can get much of the same tax deferral by buying stocks with little or no dividend payouts (or mutual funds that behave the same way) and hanging onto them for a few years. You don't pay tax until you sell. And then, if something like the current law is still in effect, you pay at a low rate.

Computing basis and sale price

The *basis* of an asset is what you paid for it, plus transaction expenses. The *sale price* is what you receive, minus expenses. The *capital gain* (or loss) is the difference between these two. In computing a gain or loss, remember to include any commissions or other fees you pay when buying and selling a stock.

If you buy 100 shares of Stock XYZ at $50 a share with a commission of $20, your basis is $5,020 (100 times $50, plus $20.) If you sell the shares at $60, again with a commission of $20, the sale price is $5,880 (100 times $60, minus $20). That gives you a capital gain of $860.

A desktop financial program such as Quicken or Microsoft Money remembers these details for you, as long as you give it complete data. When you enter buys or sells and include the commissions (plus the small federal tax on sales), Quicken automatically adds these to the purchase amount and deducts them from the sale proceeds.

Computing the holding period

When should you sell? The answer depends on the price, your own need for the money and, to some degree, the taxes you'd have to pay. If you have your transaction history in the computer and close at hand, at least you'll have no trouble telling whether you're sitting on a long-term or short-term gain. That knowledge could make the decision to sell easier.

Figuring out the holding period is easy for securities you buy and sell in single transactions. If you bought all your shares of stock XYZ on June 1, 1999, and sell all of them on July 1, 2000, you have a long-term gain (if you've made money), because you've held the shares more than a year.

But what if you bought ABC in several batches — on May 1, 1999, September 1, 1999, and February 1, 2000? With mutual funds, buying in batches is standard procedure. Even if you're not investing in funds with regular purchases, you still can expect to record purchases if you reinvest dividends and capital gains. When you sell, you might have a mix of short-term and long-term gains, not to mention multiple cost bases.

For example, say you buy the XYZ Mutual Fund in two large installments during 1999. The first was on February 1, 1999, and the second on June 7, 1999. If you sell all the shares before February 1, 2000, all the gains are short term. If you sell them after June 7, 2000, they're all long-term (except for some reinvested distributions near the end of 1999).

In between, the sale proceeds have to be divided into short- and long-term lots. This is data that you as the seller can use to decide whether you should wait.

Creating Tax Reports

A report on your year-to-date capital gains or losses can be useful even outside of the normal tax season. It can help you compute estimated taxes, for instance, and it can aid you with year-end tax decisions. Or, if you've racked up big short-term gains that push you into a higher tax bracket, you might want to offset them by realizing a loss on one of the loser stocks in your portfolio.

To get a quick read on your gains and losses with Quicken:

1. Pull down the Reports menu on the starting page and choose Taxes⇨Capital Gains Report.

A year-to-date report appears, with gains and losses on each sale of stocks or funds.

Short term gains and losses are listed first. The sales price and basis are adjusted for transaction costs.

2. Scroll down the report to see the total net short-term gain or loss, followed by long-term gains and losses.

When it comes time to fill out taxes, this data will be the basis for computing your capital gains taxes on Schedule D.

If you've managed to have a new loss for the year, there's a small silver lining. Up to $3,000 of that ($1,500 if you're married filing separately) can be deducted from your ordinary income. If you've lost more than $3,000, you can carry over the remainder to future tax years.

Online Help

The Web has some good sites that provide investor-oriented tax news and tips (the number and range of sites that deal with taxes in general is vast — far beyond the scope of this book). All the following are worth a look:

✔ **Vanguard Tax Center** (www.vanguard.com): Go to the Vanguard Group home page and click the Tax Center link under the heading Site Highlights. The top of the page has links to tax news. Scroll down to the educational links in the Tax-Smart Investing Resources section.

✔ **Yahoo! Tax Guide for Investors** (www.taxes.yahoo.com/fairmark.html): Check out links to articles on topics, such as estimated tax, Roth IRAs, and custodial accounts.

✔ **Quicken.com Investor Tax Center** (www.quicken.com/taxes/investing): Visit Quicken.com for advice, investment tips (such as a list of mutual funds with high after-tax returns) and calculators that you can use on a portfolio list at the Quicken.com site.

✔ **Bloomberg Tax Guide** (www.bloomberg.com/tax/index.html): This site has tax tips and articles on developments in tax law. You can also download and print tax forms here. See the link under the heading Tax Forms.

✔ **The IRS** (www.irs.gov): Sure, they may be eyeing your Wall Street winnings like hungry wolves. But there's something to be said for going to the source. If you've got questions, the Internal Revenue Service has the authoritative answers. It is also a good source for forms (downloadable and browsable) and information on electronic filing. Two pages on the site are worth special mention:

- Forms and Publications (www.irs.gov/forms_pubs) has links to printable forms and instructions of every type.

- Electronic Services (www.irs.gov/elec_svs) has links to pages explaining the e-filing process. Start with the link <u>IRS E-file for Individual Taxpayers</u>.

Taxes and Investment Planning

Taxes are always part of the picture when you're setting investment goals.

Financenter, which has calculators for all kinds of financial-planning questions, has several that are specific to tax impacts and tax-deferred investing:

1. Go to the home page at www.financenter.com.

2. Click <u>ClickCalcs</u> to call up a series of pull-down menus.

Look in these menus for calculators of particular interest to tax-conscious investors:

- **Retirement.** Choose How Much Can I Invest before Taxes Each Year? or What Happens if Tax Laws Change? Both take you to a form on which you fill in estimates of income, savings, amount set aside in taxable and tax deferred accounts. *See also* Part I for more on this grid.

- **Roth IRA.** The calculators in this menu, among other things, project Roth IRA returns, compare Roth and regular IRAs, and look at their suitability in estate planning.

- **Savings.** Pick How Will Taxes and Inflation Affect My Savings? for a simple calculation that shows the real rate of return, based on a nominal percentage rate, tax rates, and inflation forecasts of your choice.

- **Mutual Funds.** Try Should I Sell before or after One Year? to see the impact of capital gains taxes (as well as sales loads) on a mutual fund sale.

- **Bonds.** To see the difference a day makes in after-tax returns, go to From a Tax Standpoint when Should I Sell? This shows how holding a bond past one year cuts the tax bite (the lesson applies to stocks, too).

  Another calculator in this menu — Which Are Better, Taxable or Tax-exempt Bonds? — lets you compare the after-tax returns based on realistic interest rates (higher for the taxable bond), your tax rate, and other factors.

Investor Web Sites

The Internet is a mighty roomy place, but online businesses have been doing their best to fill it up with advice, data, and chat for the online investor. That gives you plenty to read — thousands of links covering just about every conceivable investment topic.

Remember: Although you find plenty of people talking at you on the Internet, you can tune out most of them when it comes time to do real research. The truly useful data comes from relatively few primary sources, including the Securities and Exchange Commission's EDGAR system, newswires, company reports, and finance-oriented news organizations.

In an effort to make the Web a bit more manageable, here are some sites worth visiting (and bookmarking) for their news, views, data, and analytic tools. All are free, though some offer extra services to paid subscribers.

In this part. . .

Charting

All investor home pages offer charts with basic price-action data and at least a few extras. The following are sites that specialize in more elaborate charts, which you can customize from a menu of technical indicators. Some features may require registration and log-in.

- **ASK Research** (www.askresearch.com): Click <u>Daily Charts</u> or <u>Intraday Charts</u>.

- **Big Charts** (www.bigcharts.com): After entering a stock symbol, click <u>Interactive Charting</u>.

- **ClearStation** (www.clearstation.com): After entering a symbol and clicking <u>Get Graphs!</u>, click <u>Interactive Graph Tool</u>.

Company Research

Here are sites of two kinds — those that provide a quick but comprehensive overview of a company, and those that lead you deeper into the corporate data and specialized topics.

Most of the sites here combine both functions, providing a snapshot with easy links to the historical and financial background. Some cover specialized areas, such as Insider Trader (insiders' buying and selling) and Multex Investor (analyst research).

- **Company Sleuth** (www.company.sleuth.com)

- **EDGAR** (www.sec.gov): Click the <u>Search EDGAR Archives</u> link.

- **EDGAR Online** (www.edgar-online.com)

- **FreeEDGAR** (www.freeedgar.com)

- **Hoover's Online** (www.hoovers.com)

- **Insider Trader** (www.insidertrader.com)

- **Market Guide** (www.marketguide.com)

- **Multex Investor** (www.multexinvestor.com)

- **Online Investor.com** (www.magnetsearch.com/cgi-pub/template.pl)

In addition to these sites, you can get research snapshots and links to more at the investor home pages listed earlier in this section. One of the best overviews is Profile pages at Yahoo! Finance. (Just click <u>Profile</u> on a quote for a stock.) These give an overview of company basics with links to analyst estimates, insider trades, and much more. Look for similar items when you call up a stock quote on a company at MSN Investor.

Directories

Here are two sites that list and categorize investor-oriented Web pages — thousands of them, in dozens of categories and sub-categories. I also include a third site that lists the many business- and investment-focused search engines.

- ✔ **Best of the Web** (www.investorama.com/directory/index.html)

- ✔ **Yahoo! Finance and Investing** (www.finance.yahoo.com)

- ✔ **Search Engine Guide** (www.searchengineguide.com)

Education and Advice

You don't need any help finding investment advice and opinions on the Web. These jump out at you from every portal, news outlet, and message board. But a few sites do distinguish themselves by explaining investment fundamentals and offering well-argued strategies.

Here are some good free sites for furthering your education and getting varied viewpoints on the market. One of them — TheStreet.com — also has news and commentary for paid subscribers, but its Investing Basics feature is free:

- ✔ **Alliance for Investor Education** (www.investoreducation.org)

- ✔ **CBS MarketWatch Investor's Primer** (cbs.marketwatch.com/news/primer)

- ✔ **Financenter Personal Finance & Calculators** (www.financenter.com)

- ✔ **The Motley Fool** (www.fool.com)

- ✔ **InvestorWords** (www.investorwords.com)

- ✔ **MSN Investor Insight** (moneycentral.msn.com/articles/newtoday.asp)

- ✔ **National Association of Investors Corp.** (www.better-investing.org)

- ✔ **NASDAQ Investor Services** (www.nasdaq.com/services/services.stm)

- ✓ **Sensible-Investor** (www.sensible-investor.com)

- ✓ **TheStreet.com** (www.thestreet.com)

- ✓ **Stocks at About.com** (www.stocks.about.com/finance/stocks)

- ✓ **Worldlyinvestor.com** (www.worldlyinvestor.com)

- ✓ **Yahoo! Financial Glossary** (www.biz.yahoo.com/f/g/g.html)

In addition to these sites, many online brokerages have extensive education features, open to visitors as well as customers. For an example, go to E*Trade's tutorial site at www.etrade.com (click the Knowledge Center link under the Investing heading).

Investor Home Pages

These sites are one-stop shops for online investing information and tools you need. All have quotes, charting, news on the market and individual stocks, reports on analyst research, insider trades, and much more. Some have added features for paid subscribers.

- ✓ **123Jump** (www.123jump.com)

- ✓ **America Online** users: Go to the AOL Personal Finance channel.

- ✓ **Bloomberg.com** (www.bloomberg.com)

- ✓ **CBS MarketWatch** (www.cbs.marketwatch.com)

- ✓ **CNBC.com** (www.cnbc.com)

- ✓ **CNET Investor** (www.investor.cnet.com)

- ✓ **CNNfn** (www.cnnfn.com)

- ✓ **FinancialWeb** (www.financialweb.com)

- ✓ **GO Money** (money.go.com)

- ✓ **Individual Investor** (www.individualinvestor.com)

- ✓ **Investorama** (www.investorama.com)

- ✓ **Lycos Investing** (www.investing.lycos.com)

- ✓ **MSN Investor** (www.moneycentral.msn.com/investor)

- ✓ **Netscape Investing** (www.personalfinance.netscape.com/finance/investing)

- ✓ **Quicken.com Investing** (www.quicken.com/investments)

- ✔ **SmartMoney** (www.smartmoney.com)

- ✔ **Standard & Poor's Personal Wealth**
  (www.personalwealth.com)

- ✔ **Stockpoint** (www.stockpoint.com)

- ✔ **Thomson Investors Network** (www.thomsoninvest.net)

- ✔ **Wall Street City** (www.wallstreetcity.com)

- ✔ **Yahoo! Finance** (www.finance.yahoo.com or
  www.quote.yahoo.com)

In most cases, you need to register at the preceding sites to get a user name and password, but the portfolio tracking itself is free. Try out different sites to see which ones are easiest to use and update.

Investor Protection

Here are some sites to keep on hand if you want to guard against problems or, if necessary, resolve them. The NASD Regulation site is useful for checking out brokers and their firms. The SEC site, where you can file complaints, also has investor education features. The Investor Protection Trust has links to the SEC and other regulators (such as those in the NASAA).

- ✔ **Investor Protection Trust** (www.investorprotection.org)

- ✔ **NASD Regulation** (www.nasdr.com)

- ✔ **North American Securities Administrators Association**
  (www.nasaa.org)

- ✔ **U.S. Securities and Exchange Commission** (www.sec.gov)

IPOs

Here are some leading sites for research on initial public offerings, along with online brokerages that frequently make IPOs available to customers. You can also find IPO research and education links on most of the sites listed in the "Investor Home Pages" section.

For research:

- ✔ **IPO.com** (www.ipo.com)

- ✔ **IPO Central** (www.hoovers.com): Click the IPO Central link.

- ✔ **IPO Express** (www.edgar-online.com/ipoexpress)

✔ **IPOhome.com** (www.ipo-fund.com)

✔ **ipoPros.com** (www.ipopros.com)

For brokers:

✔ **DLJdirect** (www.dljdirect.com): Click the <u>IPO Center</u> link.

✔ **E*TRADE IPO Center** (www.etrade.com): Click the <u>IPOs</u> link under the Investing heading.

✔ **MercerPartners IPO Syndicate** (www.iposyndicate.com): Click the <u>IPO Center</u> link.

✔ **Wit Capital** (www.witcapital.com): Click the <u>IPOs and Other Offerings</u> link.

✔ **WR Hambrecht & Co.** (www.openipo.com)

Mutual Funds

The following sites specialize in research and education on mutual funds and other pooled investments, such as index shares. Also, the sites listed in the "Investor Home Pages" section have links to mutual-fund data. Look for links like <u>Funds</u> or <u>Mutual Funds</u> on their front-page menus.

✔ At Yahoo! Finance, you find the mutual fund link listed in the table of contents after the heading U.S. Markets.

✔ At Bloomberg.com, it's listed under the Money heading.

✔ At CNNfn, it's under the Retirement heading.

✔ At Investorama, it's under the heading Financial Guides.

To find the online site for a fund or fund family, start by calling up a quote on the fund at Yahoo! Finance and then clicking <u>Profile</u>.

✔ **Access Vanguard** (www.vanguard.com/educ/inveduc.html)

✔ **Closed-end Fund Association** (www.closed-endfunds.com)

✔ **Index Shares Overview (American Stock Exchange)** (www.amex.com/indexshares/index_shares_over.stm)

✔ **Morningstar.com** (www.morningstar.com)

✔ **Mutual Fund Investor's Center** (www.mfea.com)

Online Communities

Message boards are no place to get your facts, but they can give you some insight into investor sentiment, and they can produce some lively exchanges of views. Here are some of the more active ones, where you are likely to find fairly current discussions even on stocks that aren't big names in the news.

- ✔ **ClearStation** (www.clearstation.com): After calling up a chart on a stock, click the <u>Discussion</u> or <u>Member Recommendations</u> links.

- ✔ **Investorville** (www.investorville.com)

- ✔ **The Motley Fool Message Boards** (www.boards.fool.com)

- ✔ **Raging Bull** (www.ragingbull.com): A chart on the front page shows the most active message boards.

- ✔ **Stock Talk** (www.siliconinvestor.com/stocktalk)

Investor home pages have some busy boards, too.

- ✔ At Yahoo! Finance, click <u>Msgs</u> in the More Info section of any quote.

- ✔ At CBS MarketWatch's "Wealth Club," click <u>Discussion</u> on the front-page menu for plenty of groups and a weekly poll asking members to play analyst and rate a stock.

- ✔ At Quicken.com, click <u>Boards</u> for logs of members' "community ratings" of stocks.

Quotes

In addition to the quotes found at all investor home pages, brokerages and many other Web pages, the following sites take quotes a bit beyond the ordinary. They offer free "streaming" quotes (that change with each trade, as you watch) or quotes on after-hours trading.

- ✔ **Datek Online Streamer** (www.datek.com): Click <u>Streamer</u> for real-time quotes for up to 10 stocks; registration required.

- ✔ **Island Book Viewer** (www.island.com/BookViewer): Check out the continually updated book of buy and sell orders at the Island ECN; available all day, but best for after-hours trading.

- ✔ **LiveCharts** (www.quote.com/quotecom/livecharts): See the graphic display of delayed quotes for stocks with real-time market indexes.

Real-time quotes are available to registered users at most investor home pages, though these often don't show as much data as the delayed "detailed" quotes at the same sites.

Stock and Fund Screens

Online screens for selecting stocks and mutual funds range from the ready-made (and very simple) to complex, custom tools that require quite a bit of financial sophistication to operate.

At financial home pages, you can find pre-defined screens:

- ✔ At MSN Investor, click the <u>Finder</u> link at the home page.

- ✔ At Quicken.com, click <u>Stock Search</u> or <u>Fund Finder</u>.

- ✔ At Yahoo!, click the <u>Finance Stock Screener</u> link under the Research heading.

See also Parts III and VII for more on these and similar tools, including mutual fund screens at Morningstar.com.

Here are some screening programs for investors who want to be able to plug in plenty of variables:

- ✔ **CNBC Fund Screener** (www.cnbc.com): Click <u>Tools</u> and then click <u>Fund Screener</u>. For custom searching, click <u>Advanced Search</u>.

- ✔ **CNBC Stock Screener** (www.cnbc.com): Click <u>Tools</u> and then click <u>Stock Screener</u>.

- ✔ **Hoover's StockScreener** (www.hoovers.com/search/forms/stockscreener)

- ✔ **Market Guide screens** (www.marketguide.com): Click <u>Screening</u>. The <u>NetScreen</u> link takes you to the simpler custom search. Click <u>StockQuest</u> for a more complex search using downloadable software.

- ✔ **MSN custom searches** (www.moneycentral.msn.com/investor): Click the <u>Finder</u> link and then click <u>Custom Search</u>.

- ✔ **Quicken advanced searches** (www.quicken.com/investments): Click <u>Stock Search</u> or <u>Fund Finder</u> and then click <u>Full Search</u>.

- ✔ **Wall Street City searches** (www.wallstreetcity.com): Click <u>Search for an Investment</u> in the left-hand menu and then click one of the links under the Best and Worst Lists heading. A premium product, <u>ProSearch</u>, is also on this page.

Glossary: Tech Talk

10-K: An annual company report, including financial data, filed with the SEC.

10-Q: A quarterly report, including financial data, filed with the SEC.

12b-1 fee: An annual fee charged by some mutual funds for marketing and distribution expenses.

after-hours trading: Buying and selling of stocks outside exchanges and outside the exchange hours. *See electronic communications network.*

alpha: A measure of a mutual fund's performance relative to the general market. An alpha over zero means the fund's return, adjusted for risk *(beta),* did better than the market.

American Stock Exchange: The second-largest floor-based stock exchange in the U.S., and the venue for trading index shares. *See index shares.*

AMEX: *See American Stock Exchange.*

annualized return: Total return of a stock or fund expressed as an annual average. The standard method of comparing securities to an index. *See total return, index.*

ask: The price at which sellers offer a security. Also known as the *offer* or *asking price. See bid, quote.*

asset allocation: Choosing a mix of investment types (such as stocks, bonds, or cash) that fits an investor's needs and tolerance for risk.

balance sheet: The section of a company's financial report that shows its assets, debts, and net worth at a point in time. *See book value, current ratio, equity.*

basis: *See cost basis.*

bear: An investor who believes prices will go down. He or she sets the tone of a *bear market,* which is marked by a prolonged and deep fall in values. *See bull.*

beta: A measure of a stock or mutual fund's price volatility (hence, its short-term risk) in comparison to the general market. A beta of 1.0 means the security's price fluctuates no more or less than a market index. *See alpha.*

bid: The price offered by buyers of a security. *See ask, quote.*

bond: An interest-bearing security that obligates its issuer to pay back a borrowed amount at a specific date. Investors commonly buy bonds issued by the U.S. government, state and local governments, foreign nations, corporations, and private entities sponsored by the federal government. *See coupon, maturity, par value,* and *yield.*

book: A term for the list of buy and sell orders on a security.

book value: A measure of the underlying value of a company's assets minus its liabilities. Normally seen as a per-share figure, it's used in *value investing* to find under-priced stocks.

breakout: Upward price movement that takes a stock's value past an older high.

bull: An investor who believes that prices are going to rise. He or she sets the tone in a *bull market,* which is marked by a sustained rise in stock values. *See bear.*

buying power: The maximum that an investor can buy at any given time in a *margin account.* It includes any available cash and the amount that can be borrowed against securities the investor owns.

call: An *option* allowing an investor to buy a stock at a certain price (the "strike" price) before a specified date. *See put.*

capital gain: The profit from the sale of an asset such as a stock, mutual fund, bond, or real estate. It's the difference between the sale proceeds and the *cost basis. Short-term capital gains,* from assets held a year or less, are taxed as ordinary income. *Long-term capital gains,* from assets held more than one year, are taxed at lower rates than ordinary income. *See cost basis, holding period.*

cash: Money available for investment. In a brokerage account, cash is typically held in a *money market fund* or an interest-bearing account.

cash account: A brokerage account allowing purchases only from the available cash balance. Unlike a *margin account,* it does not allow borrowing to buy securities.

cash flow: On a company's *income statement,* the profit before non-cash expenses (such as depreciation) are taken out. *Operating cash* flow, a variation on this, excludes interest and tax expenses as well. It's also known by the acronym *EBITDA,* for "earnings before interest, taxes, depreciation and amortization."

CD: *See certificate of deposit.*

certificate of deposit: An interest-bearing bank account, which promises repayment of a specified amount by a certain date and penalizes the holder for cashing it in early.

closed-end: *See mutual fund.*

closing price: The price of a stock at the end of the regular stock market trading session. It's usually the basis for computing the next day's gain or loss. *See after-hours trading.*

conditional offer: An offer to buy shares in an upcoming public offering. Before it becomes a firm offer, it must be reconfirmed when the new shares are *priced. See public offering, initial public offering.*

coupon: The interest rate stated on a *bond.* It can be lower or higher than the bond's actual *yield,* depending on whether the bond's price has risen or fallen from its *par value.*

cost basis: The total cost of an asset, used to compute a *capital gain.* Includes commissions or other transaction costs as well as the price of the asset when bought.

CUSIP number: A unique number given to each issue of publicly traded securities. It stands for "Committee on Uniform Securities Identification Procedures."

current ratio: On a *balance sheet,* the current assets divided by current liabilities. Current assets include cash on hand and any assets (property, receivables) that will be converted to cash within a year. Current liabilities are debts that must be paid within a year.

date of record: The date at which a shareholder must own a stock in order to be entitled to its dividend.

DIAMONDs: *Index shares* made up of stocks in the *Dow Jones Industrial Average.* Traded on the *American Stock Exchange.*

diluted EPS: *See earnings per share.*

direct stock plan: Also known as a *DSP* or "direct stock purchase plan." A plan enabling investors to buy shares directly from a company, without going through brokers.

distribution: In a mutual fund, the payment (usually annual) of dividends and/or capital gains. Any income the fund has received from dividends or the sale of stocks and bonds is usually passed on to shareholders.

dividend: A portion of a company's profit paid out to shareholders, usually on a quarterly basis. Many companies pay no dividends, preferring to reinvest all their earnings for future growth.

dividend reinvestment plan: Also known as a *DRIP.* A plan that enables shareholders of a company to take dividends in shares of stock rather than cash.

dollar-cost averaging: Investment of the same dollar amount at regular intervals. It is usually done with mutual funds or direct stock purchase plans. Dollar-cost averaging smooths out market fluctuations by making the investor buy more shares when prices are lower, and fewer when they're higher.

Dow Jones Industrial Average: A stock average based on the prices of 30 leading U.S. companies. The most widely reported of all stock indexes.

DRIP: *See dividend reinvestment plan.*

DSP: *See direct stock plan.*

earnings per share: A company's *net income* divided by the number of *shares outstanding.* Also known as *EPS,* it is reported both quarterly and annually; the annual figure is the basis for the *price-earnings ratio.* Basic EPS is the per-share net income before adjustments for new shares that might come on the market from the exercise of stock options and conversions of other securities into *common stock.* These factors are used to compute *diluted EPS,* which is the figure normally cited by analysts and financial reporters.

EBITDA: *See cash flow.*

ECN: *See electronic communications network.*

EDGAR: The *Securities and Exchange Commission's* system of online access to corporate filings. It stands for Electronic Data Gathering, Analysis, and Retrieval. It's available through the SEC's Web site or commercial services such as EDGAR Online.

electronic communications network: Also known as *ECN.* A computerized system that matches buyers and sellers of stock outside exchanges and outside regular exchange hours.

EPS: *See earnings per share.*

equity: The net worth of a company — its assets minus its debts. Also known as *shareholder's equity.*

ex-dividend: The designation for a stock that has passed its *date of record* for an upcoming dividend. Investors who buy during this period are not entitled to the dividend.

expense ratio: A mutual fund's overall expenses as a percentage of its *net asset value.* Expense ratios range from small fractions of a percent for index funds to more than 2 percent for actively managed funds.

Federal Reserve: The U.S. government agency that oversees banking and regulates the money supply. It influences stock and bond prices through its control of key interest rates.

flipping: The quick sale of shares by investors who received them in a *public offering.*

float: The number of a company's shares available for public trading. *See shares outstanding.*

forward P/E: *See price-earnings ratio.*

fundamental: A type of analysis focused on the quality of the company and its business outlook rather than the price and volume action of its stock.

gross margin: A company's *gross profit,* stated as a percentage of *net sales.*

gross profit: A company's *net sales* minus the direct costs (such as labor and raw materials) of producing goods or services. *See net income.*

holding period: The time between the buying and selling of an asset for a capital gain (or loss). *See capital gain.*

HOLDRs: A new form of tradeable security, related to *index shares,* consisting of a permanent portfolio of stocks in a particular industry. Investors can liquidate HOLDRs in stages by selling each of the stock holdings individually. The acronym stands for "Holding Company Depositary Receipts."

income statement: A table in quarterly and annual reports showing company's sales, expenses, profit, and per-share income. Also called a "profit-and-loss statement."

index: An average of stock prices designed to measure value of stock market in general or some part of it. The *Dow Jones Industrial Average* is the best-known index, while the *Standard & Poor's 500* is the benchmark against which most money managers measure their performance. Dozens of indexes also have been developed to measure market sectors.

index fund: A *mutual fund* that invests in a portfolio closely matching the composition of a stock index such as the *Standard & Poor's 500.*

index shares: Tradeable shares of portfolios that are designed to match major stock indexes as closely as possible. *See SPDRs, WEBS,* and *DIAMONDs.*

indication of interest: *See conditional offer.*

industry group: A classification of stocks by business lines (such as "semiconductors" or "biotechnology"). Stocks often rise or fall as a group in response to news or market trends. *See sector.*

initial public offering: A company's first offering of shares for public trading. Also known as an *IPO.*

insider: An executive, director, or major investor in a company who must disclose any significant trading of the firm's stock. Investors watch for unusual buying or selling patterns as clues to future performance.

institution: A mutual fund, pension fund, bank, insurance company, or other organization that buys and sells large volumes of securities. It's also called "institutional investor," and contrasted with "individual investors" — members of the public who (usually) trade in smaller amounts.

investment bank: A firm that brings new issues of stocks and bonds to market. Investment banks typically join together in syndicates to act as underwriters of public offerings, guaranteeing a price to the issuing company in exchange for a fee.

IPO: *See initial public offering.*

junk bond: *See high-yield bond.*

large cap: *See market capitalization.*

limit order: An order to buy or sell a security at a stated price or better. In a limit buy order, the investor tells the broker to pay no more than the *limit price*. In a sale, the limit price is the lowest the broker is allowed to accept.

limit price: *See limit order.*

load: In a mutual fund, a sales fee charged either on the purchase of shares or on their sale. "No-load funds" are sold without these charges. *See 12b-1 fee.*

lock-up: The period after an *initial public offering* in which major shareholders of a company are barred from selling their own stock in the company.

long-term capital gains: *See capital gains.*

long-term debt: On a *balance sheet,* any debt or other obligation due in more than one year.

MACD: *See moving average convergence/divergence.*

margin: In investing, the buying of stocks, bonds, or other securities with money borrowed from a broker, and with other "marginable" securities in the investor's account used as collateral.

margin account: A brokerage account that permits margin trading. *See cash account.*

margin rate: The interest rate charged by brokers on money they lend investors to buy stocks on margin.

market capitalization: The total stock-market value of a company. It's the current stock price multiplied by the number of *shares outstanding.* Analysts usually divide stocks into three market-cap classes. Stocks with market caps under $1 billion are usually called *small cap.* Stocks up to $5 billion usually fall in the *mid-cap* range. The rest are *large-cap* stocks.

market order: An order to buy or sell a security as soon as possible at the best available price.

market risk: The risk of a security rising or falling in value. In bonds, market risk comes from the threat of rising interest rates, which force the value of the bond down as they force the *yield up.* Credit risk, on the other hand, is the possibility that the borrower may not be able to pay the interest and principal.

maturity: The date on which a bond's principal must be repaid.

mid-cap: *See market capitalization.*

minimum maintenance: The minimum level of equity — cash and securities' market value, minus debt — that investors must have in a margin account. If the value of securities falls below this level, a "margin call" goes out. The investor then has to add money to the account or sell securities to beef up the equity.

momentum investing: A method of stock analysis based on the idea of following current price and volume trends. A momentum investor buys a stock in a clear uptrend with heavy volume, and sells out of stocks falling on heavy volume.

money market fund: A form of *mutual fund* with a portfolio of short-term debt (the maturities usually no more than a few months). It is designed to maintain a constant asset value and preserve capital.

moving average: A method of showing longer-term trends amid shorter-term fluctuations. A 50-day moving average, for instance, shows the average price on each day for the preceding 50 trading days.

moving average convergence/divergence: Known as *MACD*, this is a tool of technical analysis showing the interplay between two moving averages, one longer-term than the other. Analysts watch for points at which the shorter-term ("faster") moving average crosses the longer-term ("slower") one or diverges from it.

municipal bond: A bond issued by a state or local government. Its interest is *tax-exempt* as long as it is not used to benefit a private party.

mutual fund: A pool of stocks and/or bonds in which the investors can buy shares. Funds come in two types: *Open-end* funds (more common) create new shares on demand and sell them directly to investors. *Closed-end* funds issue a fixed number of shares that are traded on an exchange.

NASDAQ Stock Market: A computerized network providing dealers with prices on thousands of stocks traded "over-the-counter" — that is, not through a trading-floor exchange such as the *AMEX* or the *New York Stock Exchange*. Its listings include most of the large-cap leaders in technology and the Internet. NASDAQ stands for National Association of Securities Dealers Automated Quotations system.

NASDAQ Composite: A stock *index* that tracks the *NASDAQ Stock Market*.

NAV: *See net asset value.*

net asset value: The per-share value of an *open-end mutual fund*. Computed at the end of each trading day, it's the total value of the fund's holdings (including cash) divided by the number of shares. *See public offering price.*

net income (or loss): In an *income statement,* the profit (or loss) left after all expenses are subtracted from sales. Also called the "bottom line," it's the basis of *earnings per share.* Quarterly net income is usually compared to the income for the corresponding quarter of the previous year.

net margin: *Net income* as a percentage of *net sales.*

net sales: A company's total sales after deductions for returns or discounts. This is the standard "top line" revenue figure.

New York Stock Exchange: The largest stock exchange in the world, where shares of most of the world's largest companies are traded.

no-load mutual fund: *See load.*

odd lot: A trading unit of stock shares not divisible by 100. *See round lot.*

offer: *See ask.*

open-end: *See mutual fund.*

operating income (or loss): In an *income statement*, the profit (or loss) after expenses connected with the normal operation of a company's business. It excludes interest, taxes, and non-recurring costs.

operating margin: *Operating income* as a percentage of *net sales.*

options: Securities (part of a class called "derivatives") that allow holders to buy or sell stocks at specified prices. *See calls, puts.*

par value: The face value of a stock or bond. It has no relation to market value and is usually much lower.

P/E: *See price-earnings ratio.*

PEG: *See price/earnings to growth ratio.*

POP: *See public offering price.*

price-earnings ratio: The price of a company's stock divided by its annual *earnings per share.* Shortened to *P/E* or *PE*, it's usually based on the *EPS* of the most recent four quarters.

price/earnings to growth ratio: A stock's *price-earnings ratio* compared to its annual growth rate (usually in earnings). Called PEG for short, this ratio is used to identify companies that may be relatively cheap in relation to their past or projected growth rates.

pricing: In an *initial public offering,* the final setting of the price that investors will pay to the issuing company for the new shares. Investors who made *conditional offers* earlier are asked at this point to reconfirm them.

prospectus: A document disclosing details of an investment — such as a stock issue or a mutual fund — to prospective investors. It is required in any offer of shares to the public.

public offering: The issue of new shares for trading by the general public.

public offering price: In an *open-end mutual fund*, the per-share price paid by buyers. In a no-load fund, it's the same as the *net asset value.* In a fund with an front-end sales charge, that "load" is added to the NAV.

put: An *option* allowing the holder to sell a security at a stated price before a specified deadline. As with *short sales*, put options are a way to make money from declining stock prices.

quick ratio: On a *balance sheet,* the company's *liquid* current assets — cash, marketable securities, and receivables minus inventory — divided by its current liabilities. This ratio answers the question of whether the company could pull through if sales suddenly dried up.

quiet period: A time before and after a public offering during which a company is barred from publicly promoting its shares.

quotation: *See quote.*

quote: Short for *quotation*. The current *bid* and *ask* prices of a stock, along with the price of the last sale. Online quotes usually add several items of information to this basic data, including the change from the previous closing price, the volume and high and low for the day. *See bid, ask, quoted price, spread.*

quoted price: The latest price at which a stock was sold.

real-time quote: A stock quote showing the latest prices without the usual delay imposed on issues (15 to 20 minutes). Indexes such as the *Dow Jones Industrial Average* and the *NASDAQ Composite* are always quoted in real time.

registration statement: *See S-1.*

relative strength: A stock's price performance compared to the general market (usually as measured by the *Standard & Poor's 500*). Relative strength is usually stated as a percentile figure, with 99 being the highest.

resistance: A technical term for a price level toward which a stock repeatedly rises, only to fall back. *See breakout.*

return on equity: *Net income* as a percentage of a company's net worth or *shareholder's equity*. A key measure of profitability.

revenue: *See net sales.*

round lot: A number of shares divisible by 100.

S&P 500: *See Standard & Poor's 500.*

SEC: *See Securities and Exchange Commission.*

secondary offering: A *public offering* of shares previously issued by a company but not publicly traded.

sector fund: A *mutual fund* specializing in stocks of an industry or broad market *sector,* such as biotechnology, software, or the technology industry as a whole.

Securities and Exchange Commission: The federal agency that oversees the issuing and trading of stocks, bonds, and other securities in the U.S.

settlement: Payment to cover the cost of a securities purchase. Investors have three business days to deposit funds with a broker if they don't already have enough cash in their accounts.

shares outstanding: The total number of shares issued by a company, including shares not registered for public trading. *See float.*

shareholders' equity: *See equity.*

short sale: The selling of shares, borrowed from a broker, to buy back and return later, hopefully at a lower price.

short-term capital gains: *See capital gains.*

small cap: *See market capitalization.*

S-1: The registration document for an *initial public offering.* It contains a detailed description of the company, its competitive position, and its risks, along with financial information.

SEC: *See Securities and Exchange Commission.*

SPDRs: Short for Standard & Poor's Depositary Receipts. *AMEX*-traded *index shares* that mirror the *Standard & Poor's 500.*

spread: The difference between *bid* and *ask* prices.

Standard & Poor's 500: An *index* that follows the stocks of 500 leading publicly traded companies in the U.S. In general, these are the 500 largest companies by *market capitalization.*

stock: A share of ownership in a business. Most stocks traded online are "common stocks." "Preferred stocks," fewer in number, have first crack at dividends.

stock exchange: An organized marketplace in which shares of stocks, bonds, or options are bought and sold. The *New York Stock Exchange, AMEX,* and regional exchanges have a physical location, including a "trading floor," where members trade on their own accounts and on behalf of others.

stop order: An order to trade a stock after it has reached a prescribed *stop price.* At that point, the broker must buy or sell the stock at the best available price, as in a *market order.*

stop-limit order: An order to buy or sell a stock once it has reached a certain price, and then to sell it at a prescribed limit price or better.

street name: Registration of shares in the name of a broker rather than the owner. This makes it easy to buy and sell (that is, transfer ownership).

support: In technical analysis, a price that seems to mark the lower limit of a stock's fluctuations. *See resistance.*

tax-deferred: Free from taxes now, but taxable at a later date. Capital gains and other earnings in most tax-deferred retirement accounts, such as traditional IRAs and 401(k)s, are not taxed until the holder starts withdrawing the money in retirement.

tax-exempt: Free from taxes, now and in the future. Earnings from Roth IRAs and interest from public-purpose *municipal bonds* are tax-exempt.

technical: Analysis of stocks by price and volume patterns, especially as revealed through charts.

tick: The price movement of a stock on its last trade. An uptick means the stock rose at the last sale; a downtick means it fell.

trading symbol: A symbol of one to five letters identifying a stock or mutual fund and used in all online trading.

trailing P/E: *See price-earnings ratio.*

Treasury bill: Debt issued by the U.S. Treasury with a maturity of one year or less.

Treasury bond: Treasury debt with a maturity of 10 years or more.

Treasury note: Treasury debt with a maturity between one and 10 years.

trading range: A price pattern marked by a consistent *support* level at the bottom and *resistance* at the top.

turnover: In a mutual fund, the rate at which the fund's managers buy and sell securities. A turnover of 100 (or 100 percent) means that an amount equal to the total value of the portfolio changes hands in the course of a year.

underwriter: *See investment bank.*

value investing: An investing strategy of looking for companies that appear undervalued in relation to their earnings and assets. Value investors tend to focus on low PE and price-to-book value ratios rather than rapid growth.

WEBS: Short for World Equity Benchmark Securities, these are *index shares* made up of stocks in various overseas markets. They are traded on the *AMEX*.

whisper number: An informal, unpublished earnings estimate that makes the rounds of stock traders shortly before a company announces its quarterly results.

yield: The interest on a bond as a percentage of its current price.

yield curve: A graph comparing *yields* on Treasury bills, notes, and bonds. It shows how yields rise or fall with maturities. In a "normal" yield curve, yields are higher for longer maturities (reflecting the greater *market risk*). On an "inverted" curve, they're higher at the short end.

zero-coupon bond: A bond paying no cash interest. It is bought at a discount from its face value, which is paid at maturity.

Index